HOW TO FISH STREAMS

HOW TO FISH STREAMS

Dave Bowring

WINCHESTER PRESS

Library of Congress Cataloging in Publication Data

Bowring, Dave.
How to fish streams.

Includes index.
1. Fishing. I. Title.
SH441.B63 799.1'2 77-1863
ISBN 0-87691-197-1

Published by Winchester Press
205 East 42nd Street
New York, N.Y. 10017

Printed in the United States of America

DEDICATION

To Bob Daily and Harold Barefoot, who showed me where. To all the thousands of battlers fighting to keep free waters free, who showed me it can be done. And to my father, who, in the beginning, showed me why.

CONTENTS

FOREWORD

Obviously Dave Bowring is never going to be President of these United States. Readers of this book will soon realize Dave wasted far too many of his early days to prepare for the office. Instead he spent his energies with cane pole and worms outwitting sunfish and bullheads in streams close to home. And he has been fishing ever since.

Dave has written a book for every angler who has or will someday fish a North American stream. The text's platform has a happy and much needed bias against purists. The author shows little patience for those who feel there is only one way to catch fish. Instead his suggestions are reminiscent of the backup systems used in space exploration. Dave always suggests a number of backup angling systems whether it has to do with carp or trout.

In short, this book is definitely not for stuffy, single-minded anglers who glory in being narrow-minded about their sport. Rather it is intended for the vast majority of stream fishermen who are a lot less interested in minute fly patterns than how to put fillets in the kitchen skillet. The book campaigns against anglers who make up silly rules.

Dave's statements about the immense variety of options the stream fisherman has in tackle include just about everything except trotlines, jugs, and hand grenades. But one has the suspicion that if the author were faced with the dilemma of using one of these methods, and all were legal, he would use them with enthusiasm. Dave may tell you he prefers a small fiberglass canoe to one made of aluminum because of the noise factor. But when the smoke clears, the reader can assume that Dave would fish out of a tin bathtub, if that's all that was available.

It might be a good idea to read the last chapter first. Only then will you comprehend the conspiracy afoot among agencies and individuals to eliminate countless miles of streams. And hopefully you'll join Dave in lobbying to save our streams.

This foreword is herewith ended—the writer reads something in the text about smallmouth bass fishing that requires personal and immediate attention.

Karl H. Maslowski
Cincinnati, Ohio

INTRODUCTION

Why fish streams? Man-made farm ponds are far more numerous, lakes are often easier to reach and sometimes produce larger fish. Streams are temperamental when it rains and when it doesn't, are dammed, flooded, polluted, used as junk disposals and as open toilets for industries and cities. So why fish streams?

Because streams are things that none of the other waters can ever be. They are natural, they are always the same yet always changing, they hold just a little mystery around every bend, below every waterfall, and inside every eddy. Learn to fish one man-made reservoir holding bass and you can fish them all, but not so with streams. Each stream, in truth every pool and riffle of every stream, is a problem with a solution to be sought by every angler who wets his waders in its waters.

Fish a farm pond once and the experience, the knowhow, will be just as valid a year later. But let just one spring flood rearrange the deadfalls in a steelhead river, let one gravel bar wash out in your favorite smallmouth stream, and the river presents you with all new problems, all new challenges, the next time you walk its banks.

I believe streams to be romantic things, as ready to carry your daydreams as they are your dry fly or canoe. They are medicine for the soul, the highways of Lewis and Clark, the arteries of national forests, and the ever-changing yet unchanged link with a time when we didn't have air-pollution alerts and strip mining and no-swimming signs along our beaches.

If this book is anything, it is intended as a gentle guide to sportfishing in streams, not a harsh taskmaster. I hate the know-it-alls who will, if you and I let them, tell us where we will fish and how we will fish and with what. But let us, you and me, become good friends as we wade in running water, discussing as friends do the complexities of a shared pleasure and knowing all the while that it is the experience, and not the weight of our creels, that makes the effort worthwhile.

Although the word "stream" appears in the title of this book, I by no means exclude the hundreds of watercourses across the continent known as "rivers," particularly since the only difference between rivers and streams is often local nomenclature rather than geological fact. My dictionary says a stream is a steady flow of water over the earth's surface, which seems fine until one realizes that the definition applies to the Columbia, Tennessee, Hudson, and Mississippi as well as to the creek behind the barn. So let's consider a stream to be any flow of water holding enough fish to draw the odd angler, but not so large it can't be spanned by a good caster on a windless day. That's as precise a definition as we need.

This book contains, in what I hope is logical sequence, chapters on each of the major gamefish species, or common groupings of species, with tips on tackle and fishing methods especially adapted for each. May the book shorten your winters and lengthen your summers.

FISHING THE MINI-STREAMS

You've been on the water since first light and now, three hours later, the morning sun is still only halfway to its zenith. No one fishes with you, yet other fishers are about. The fading tracks of a passing raccoon are clear in the shoreline ooze, and there is the dark flash of a mink as it leaves a streamside log and swims away. The startled squawk of a green heron draws your momentary attention as the two of you meet, quite without warning, at a bend in the stream.

You meet other fishers on the waters little frequented by man, but they wear fur and feathers, and you don't mind them a bit. In fact, yours are the only boot tracks along this stream. It suffers no tin cans, no gum wrappers, no discarded tires. You are alone, and you delight in it.

Fishing the truly small streams, often called creeks or brooks, offers the discriminating angler a rare chance to fish by himself on what amounts to his own private water. He needn't fear that some mannerless oaf will splash into the pool he is fishing, and although the fish he finds are usually small, they are plentiful, unsophisticated, and good sport on the light tackle he carries.

Mini-streams, God bless 'em, are found in virtually all parts of North America. If you aren't aware of several in your home bailiwick, that only demonstrates that few know about them and fewer still wet a line there. Mini-streams are tougher to locate than major watercourses. They seldom appear on topographical maps, because of their small size, and are seldom talked about among anglers. If *you* have found your own bass or trout hotspot, do you tell others about it? Enough said.

A small limestone stream, often less than 10 feet wide, flows through a lovely hardwoods less than thirty minutes by auto from my home. The stream is spring-fed, flows over a good rock and gravel base, and has plenty of shoreline shade to maintain a reasonably cool water temperature even in midsummer. Once a few friends and I had the idea of asking the state fishery office to stock the creek with trout on an experimental basis. In order to do this, we had to walk every inch of the area to be stocked, noting pool depths, water temperatures, flow rate, and natural foods found in the water.

Out of habit, I carried an ultralight spinning rod and a handful of ⅛-ounce spinners, making the odd cast here and there between notations. When about a mile of stream had been waded—and fished—it suddenly dawned on me that I had caught and released more than a dozen fish. Most were smallmouth bass in the 10–14-inch range, plus a number of rock bass, green sunfish, and one lonely largemouth bass.

It didn't take much conversation with my companions to persuade us to withdraw our request for trout stocking on that little stream. The availability of trout would have drawn many more anglers than now fish the water and necessitated the arranging of public-fishing easements with landowners, perhaps alienating them. As it now stands, the little creek is troutless but is a pleasure to fish and wade for bass and panfish. The landowners are happy, the mink and kingfishers are still there, and for my companions and me, spending a quiet evening under the stream's canopy of cottonwoods and oaks is like being in church.

This stream, like most others falling in the mini-water classification, is so small that few motorists using nearby roads give it a second glance, and fishing it seldom if ever occurs to

The headwaters of a river. Springs are the originating waters for many of the finest trout rivers of the West.

them. But not taking creeks so lightly is something I learned early. My father never drove a car, so I had to be content to fish within walking or biking distance of home, except for the few times when a friend provided transportation. I got to know all the local waters well enough to catch fish from them, and if that meant settling for rock bass when the smallmouth weren't hitting, I was just as happy.

Gamefish found in mini-waters are there, by and large, for one of two reasons. They may be native to the creek and therefore present virtually all year, or they may be native to larger water downstream fed by the creek. These migrants are only temporarily present, either for spawning or to escape

Bob Daily watches his line intently for the touch of a fish. Trout and other species often use bottom plants as cover in streams where cover is scarce.

some downstream catastrophe, such as flooding, channelization, or a dose of pollution. Once the disturbance passes, migrant fish usually drop back down into the larger water they prefer, taking fishermen with them. Stay on the little water for a change.

The characteristics of small-stream fishing should dictate the tackle you'll choose. Such factors as relatively shallow pools, clear water, narrow shorelines, and overhanging foliage all point to light tackle and rather short rods, whether for spinning, spincasting, or flyfishing. Even that old faithful, the cane pole, is best trimmed short when used on little waters. Fish can certainly see, and in a manner of speaking they hear quite well. These senses are especially important in creek habitat, because the little waters offer far fewer avenues of escape from predators; pools are shallow and riffles are often virtually impassable in summer. Predations by fish-eating creatures are probably greater on small streams than on big rivers, simply because the fish have fewer places to run.

All this means that your tackle should permit you to present a lure or bait with an absolute minimum of disturbance to the water. It means your line must be fine enough to cast only the tiniest of shadows on the water and stream bottom, and that your tackle must be able to cast very light offerings accurately for short distances.

I have two ultralight rigs which I favor for small waters. I have caught many fish on each outfit and believe they are well suited to the purpose. The spinning outfit, all 5 feet of it, includes a soft-tipped fiberglass rod with a simple cork grip and two aluminum rings to anchor the reel in place. Five line guides of good diameter do the job without weighting the entire rod too much, and are of Carboloy construction. The reel I use is an open-bail Mitchell 308; I also have the Model 204, which is newer than the 308 and costs less. I think the choice of monofilament line for this tiny rig is especially important. The line must be of fine diameter because of the water's clarity, but it also must be tough and capable of holding up under stress and abrasion. For these reasons, I choose the softest 2- and 4-pound-test mono on the market. Soft mono offers greater abrasion resistance and knot strength than stiffer lines because it molds itself around obstacles and draws tighter when knotted. It's also handy to know that a line's advertised breaking strength is established when the line is fully saturated with water, rather than dry. This can be crucial when the line between you and the fish tests only 4 pounds or so, although virtually all modern line will hold weights considerably greater than its advertised breaking point if reel drag and rod flex are properly used.

My little fly outfit consists of a 6-foot glass rod with a soft tip (important for dry-fly fishing), a No. 5 floating line in a light color so it can be easily seen on shadowy water, and a 3-inch ultralight single-action fly reel just big enough to hold 30 yards of level line. Very few of my flycasts on small streams are longer than 30 feet, and most are shorter, so level fly line, which costs less than tapered line, does the job well. I might go to a tapered line, say a weight-forward model, when dry-fly fishing on particularly clear waters, but this is an exception.

When flycasting the mini-streams, it's a good idea to know how to throw a decent line without the luxury of a backcast, because of streamside foliage. Sidearm flips, roll casts—anything to get the business end of things on the water without disturbing the fish. In extreme cases where foliage was chokingly heavy, I've even moved upstream from the target water, gently deposited my bait in the current, and let the stream itself move the offering into spots where I believed fish to be located. This is time-consuming but presents your bait in a most natural manner. As someone once said, walk right down and start fishing the stream; if you sneak around the fish will get suspicious. . . .

In-stream cover of any type is critical when on creeks and brooks. Fish are spooky in small water, and fishing around cover lets the angler put his bait near fish without alerting his quarry. Don't pass up *any* cover—fallen logs, undercut banks, brushpiles, old drainage tiles, bridge pilings, anything.

It's also a good idea to travel that creek in an upstream direction, for a number of reasons. Most gamefish face *into* the current, because from it they obtain food, and approaching the fish from the rear is not as likely to alert it and put it off the

Big fish in snaggy water, and on ultralight tackle, too. This fellow has his hands full of winter rainbow problems.

feed. Wading anglers will not send debris dislodged by their boots over fish located upstream, and fish are easier to bring to net using the current as an aid. Also, the fighting of a hooked fish will not alert other fish in the next upstream pool.

Here's an added tip: Keep in mind that truly small streams are subject to midsummer temperature rises even more than larger watercourses, and direct, hot sun rays are as uncomfortable to the fish as they are to you and me. Fish will congregate in water in deep shadow during the hot part of the day, and this is where you should be fishing to find the fish. Make

Waterfalls provide natural barriers to migrating fish, help aerate the stream, and constantly change in form as they wear away the bedrock.

it a rule of thumb to face *into* the sun as much as possible, dropping your bait on the upstream edge of shaded water. Doing so keeps your shadow from alerting the fish you want to catch.

Mini-streams are particularly vulnerable to midsummer drought, and unless they contain a number of large-volume springs, can lose most or all of the current and oxygenation when pool levels become so reduced that little or no water flows through the riffles. For the fish, this means less living room, higher water temperatures, less dissolved oxygen, fewer hiding places, and a reduced food supply—not exactly ideal conditions. But let a good, steady shower put a new water supply in the creek, and the alert fisherman is back in business. All of a sudden, water levels are acceptable, natural

Gamefish in meadow streams and exposed brooks often seek the shade provided by overhanging trees. Such spots are always worth an exploratory cast or two. Here Pete Fusco gains a working line over Ohio's Mad River.

foods are again being carried to the fish, and the rainfall has dropped water temperatures a few degrees, all of which put fish in a feeding mood immediately.

Two readers of my outdoor column recently showed me the benefits of watching for midsummer rain. A drought of perhaps three weeks had dropped stream levels and about killed the fishing. Finally one Friday night a storm front moved in, dropping barometric pressure drastically and depositing over an inch of rain before Saturday morning. The two fishermen quickly gathered their tackle and were knee-deep in the creek at dawn on Saturday, knowing the fresh water would move fish to feed. The results were two limits of smallmouth on Saturday and a repeat performance of the same feat on Sunday morning. By early afternoon of the second day enough silt had moved into their favorite stream to cloud it too much for good fishing, but they didn't care; they already had thirty-two keeper bass on ice and were home in plenty of time to watch a Sunday-afternoon doubleheader on television.

Many of the same baits and lures which work on larger streams do well on the mini-waters, except in smaller sizes. One-inch crayfish will catch bass sooner in small waters than will 5-inch giants, and so will 1- or 2-inch minnows or redworms. Remember to keep your hook small enough to be completely hidden inside a worm, and light enough to give a small minnow or crayfish the freedom to wiggle naturally. Usually no added weight is needed when fishing a small stream with bait, because casts are quite short and pools are shallow.

Artificials for this type of fishing should also be quite small. Although you may catch bass averaging 10–15 inches long, the food those fish are used to chasing usually measures only an inch or so in length, and using baits much larger than this would undoubtedly make proper presentation impossible, anyway. For bass, I am quite devoted to ultralight spinners. These weigh from 1/8 ounce all the way down to 1/32 ounce. Spinners this small must contain clevises designed to turn the spinner blade at slow retrieve speeds, and the overall shape of the spinners must permit easy casting. Two types of spinners which fulfill these requirements are the Mepps and Panther Martin types, both of which cast well and ride well in shallow water. Color seems more a matter of personal preference to the fisherman than to the fish–if the bait is there, the fish will hit it, color aside–but spinner finish is another matter. My fishing notes indicate I catch far more small-stream fish on bronze- or copper-bladed spinners than on baits with chrome or silver blades, perhaps because the silvery metal reflects too much light and frightens wary gamefish. Bronze- and copper-bladed spinners seem to offer just enough flash, yet emit vibrations on retrieve identical to silver models. An

Well-managed areas containing streams provide for many recreational uses. Here father and son and their beagle watch another father-son team fish for winter panfish.

exception to my choice of dark-bladed spinners occurs when the water is particularly dingy or colored by rains; at such times the fish seem to require a bit more flash. I'm also sure dirty stream waters require baits to be retrieved a bit slower than at other times, with more attention to fishing closer to suspected holding water.

Tiny wobbling plugs also do well at times, particularly when fishing for rock bass and the occasional stream largemouth. Two baits which have served me well are the Fly Ike and the Midget Mudbug by Arbogast. Don't pass up the relatively new pre-rigged redworms on today's market. Only about 3 inches overall, these creations contain two or three pre-rigged flyhooks and can be very effective on rock bass, smallmouth, and panfish.

A popular quarry among early springtime anglers (the author not included) is the white sucker *(Catostomus commersonii)*. This fish forms large schools in early spring and migrates into even the smallest creeks to spawn. It is quite wary and feeds on bottom, probably explaining the most effective fishing method, which is a trotline stretched across the stream and armed with from four to a dozen or more redworm-baited hooks on 18-inch dropper lines reaching bottom. The suckers are usually smoked. Other methods of preparing these fish are futile because of their extreme boniness. A few white suckers (one of some sixty-nine species of sucker nationwide) are taken by bait fishermen angling dead on bottom.

One of the most fondly remembered creeks I ever fished ran directly beside a semi-rural road a mile or so from home. It was easily reached by walking, and I fished it every summer as a boy. I am sure hundreds of cars used that road every day, yet not once did I see another fisherman on the creek. The current was slow, even though the water flowed down a rather steep hill; its movement down the hill was a series of small waterfalls between even smaller pools lined with flat rocks, and in these small pools I found dozens of willing bullheads, called yellowbellies or catfish in those days.

Fishing for these whiskerpusses was almost too easy. All I needed was a cane pole, 6 feet of nondescript line, and a hook of any size at all. A wad of one or two nightcrawlers provided

A small canoe, a quiet river, and a few willing bass. This angler brings the fish aboard in the classic manner.

bait enough to catch half a dozen fish, provided I struck soon enough to prevent the eager fish from swallowing my hook.

Because the pools were often within 10 feet of the roadway, no doubt I was observed by countless motorists in passing autos, yet no one ever stopped to inquire into the fishing, nor did I ever see evidence of another angler on the creek. Well, come to think of it, that's not entirely true. I did run into another fisher one summer evening, a 4-foot common water snake just leaving the water with a minnow in its mouth.

I haven't fished that creek in more than twenty years, but I'll bet it's unfished yet, except perhaps by a boy with the good sense to take it seriously.

When fishing small streams where the water is especially clear, it is not unusual for the angler to be able to spot his fish before casting. This can be true when fish are rising to naturals, of course, but it's also possible when good-sized fish are holding in slick water which can be penetrated by human vision. Michigan outdoor writer and fishing guide Dave Richey told me he fishes for fall-run chinook and coho salmon by first spotting his quarry, then pulling a lure past its nose again and again until the fish takes it, probably more from annoyance than hunger. A goodly number of the streams drawing salmon from the Great Lakes and elsewhere are quite narrow, yet they produce some amazingly large fish, some over 20 pounds.

Richey has devised a way to use fly tackle on these big fish. He rigs a stout rod and reel with sinking-tip line, adding 24 inches of lead-core fly line on the end. To this is tied a 3-foot piece of heavy monofilament leader testing in the neighborhood of 15 pounds, and finally a rather large streamer, bucktail, or wet fly dressed in bright colors.

"They may not hit it the first few times you bring it past them, but do it enough and eventually they'll hit," said Richey with a grin. The grin was, no doubt, due to recollections of what it's like to battle a large, strong salmon on a mini-stream armed with just a fly rod.

Maybe the reason I enjoy small-stream fishing so much is really just a distillation of a romance with stream fishing in general. The mini-waters require many of the same skills as their downstream brethren, but just enough is different to make the small waters another game altogether.

Take the needed tackle and equipment, for example. The stream or small-river smallmouth seems quite willing to take a bait or lure hauled behind 8- or 10-pound-test line. But its creek-living counterpart would probably bury its head under some rock if such heavy line were used in all but the rare dirty-water situation. Quarter-ounce spinners might well take the larger rock bass from a limestone and mud river, but that bait must be scaled down at least by half before a mini-stream rockie will chase it.

Small-stream trout are, if anything, even *more* demanding in their requirements for light tackle, careful approach, and gossamer presentation. Lord knows I've flushed enough trout because of inept casting, such as happened two winters ago on a newly discovered (by me) tributary of a popular Midwestern trout river. The main branch of the river was in tolerable shape, but a morning of flyfishing had turned nothing. I thought it a good reason to break for lunch and meandered upstream in search of my partner.

Around a wooded bend in the stream I came across the mouth of a tributary creek, broad, flat, and sterile where it entered the river but appearing a bit more promising a few dozen yards upstream. I decided to dawdle there a bit, at least until my partner came back down the main branch for lunch.

Not far from its mouth the creek narrowed to half its original width and bent sharply right, then left around a gravel bar. The bends were clogged with brush and logs, but enough green water showed from beneath the pile to make floating a fly there worthwhile. The first cast hit the water a bit too hard as I tried to stay clear of the snags, resulting only in a dead drift and no fish. A second cast was better and drew a rising fish, up from the pile for a closer look at this oddly floating insect in the middle of winter. Another cast brought another inspection but no strike, so I changed to a weighted brown nymph and cast a fourth time, angling the cast slightly upstream and as close to the pile of debris as I could.The nymph plopped on the water and sank, hesitated a moment, and then stopped dead, my line bellying out downstream, a sure sign of a snag.

It was my only weighted nymph in brown dressing, a favored fly with several notches on its belt, and I sorely wanted to keep it. So it was hitch up the waders, haul in the slack line, and wade into the pool to hand-retrieve the bait. I had

"Streams are poetic things, as willing to carry your daydreams as they are your canoe or dry fly . . ." Courtesy Little Miami Inc.

no sooner entered the water when four rainbows, none under 10 inches long, flushed from beneath the pile and scurried around the gravel bar to undisturbed water.

Moments later, the errant nymph back in hand, I made a mental note to remember this spot. Since that winter day I have returned to that creek perhaps a dozen times, yet the only other humans I have seen there were three young boys skipping stones across the flat water near the creek mouth. As far as I know, I'm the only fisherman who leaves the main river to try the creek. And I plan to keep it that way.

In late summer, when most small waters are at their lowest level of the year, fish continue to feed on insects, but these are no longer the nymphs and aquatic insects found there earlier, but rather terrestrial creatures that have dropped, crawled, or been blown into the water from nearby trees and grasses. These insects—grasshoppers, beetles, ants, caterpillars, crickets, and moths—seldom drift farther than a few feet before being nabbed by insect-hungry fish. And if the combination of plentiful insects and hungry fish doesn't give any angler worth his sinkers an idea, well, I've been talking through my hat for several chapters.

Bushy dry flies, cork and deerhair poppers, rubber spiders, and other top-water lightweights will all take mini-stream fish in late summer, provided they are of a size approximating the real thing and are presented as similarly as possible to the way the actual insects strike the water. Artificial flies and poppers can, of course, be fished and fished well on fly tackle, but spinning enthusiasts need not be left out of this great late-season bonanza. Simply buy yourself a clear plastic spinning bubble, the kind with spring-loaded posts in each end which admit a bit of water for casting weight, and knot it about 4 feet above the end of your monofilament line. Then tie on one of these tiny floaters and drop it as lightly on the water as your rig permits. The spinning bubble appears, if anything, to be merely a real bubble on the surface to a feeding fish, and is usually ignored. The bubble method catches just as many fish as fly tackle for all but the most wary of stream fish. Try it and see.

Fishing with the live insects themselves can also produce excellent results in late summer, provided the tackle is light enough to permit the bait to move naturally. Light wire hooks are excellent for this purpose, and the finer monofilament lines can be used on almost any popular rod and reel. Just be sure you use care in impaling the insects on the hook, keeping them alive and kicking for as long as possible. Caterpillars should squirm, crickets and grasshoppers should kick, moths should flutter and kick. All of these seemingly unimportant movements send out telltale ripples which attract fish, and the more such movements your tackle allows, the more effective your bait will be. There are various ways to capture and keep live bait; they are discussed at length in another chapter.

I think the most memorable moment I ever experienced while small-stream fishing occurred years ago when I was a teenager. A canful of nightcrawlers, an old Bronson reel, and a steel casting rod were my modest tackle, and a meandering meadow stream was my intended water. A hard rain had lasted for days and ended only that morning, bringing the normally placid little brook up out of its banks in a coffee-and-cream torrent. Anyone with less enthusiasm would have packed it in and gone home, but I merely decided I'd have to work a little harder this trip, baited up with a couple of 'crawlers,' and heaved the bait into the current. The brown water swallowed the bait and it was gone from sight immediately.

After several casts of the gob, the bait suddenly stopped in midstream as if on a snag. I hauled back, the snag moved, and I was into a very heavy fish. We battled back and forth a few minutes, the fish doing most of the moving while I did most of the praying. The muddy water obscured the fish until it was nearly ashore, when I pounced on it with both hands. It made no difference to an excited and delighted youngster that the fish was a yellowish pucker-mouthed carp. It was nearly as long as my arm and weighed 9 pounds. After I'd paraded around the neighborhood with my catch it was unceremoniously buried as fertilizer in my mother's flower garden, and for all I know its enrichment helps the roses still, there behind the red brick garage.

STREAM TACTICS

Movement is the most obvious and most important difference between fishing dead water and fishing streams.

Stream and river water moves, flows, changes its bed and its route. A particular stream is the same stream it was yesterday, yet the flow is always nibbling away at gravel bars, sand banks, fallen logs, dams, and bridge abutments.

Drop a bait near fish cover in a lake or pond and it sinks where it lands, but the same bait must be dropped on the *upstream* side of stream cover or the current will sweep it down and away from any fish around that cover.

The same goes for top-feeding fish. Surfacing trout or bass in a lake demand that the bait be plopped nearly on their heads, but in top-water stream fishing the fly or plug must be cast upstream from the fish so that the current will carry it over the fish in a natural manner.

There are dozens of such examples of why the consistently successful stream fisherman uses different tactics when astream than does his lake-fishing counterpart. The fish, and the stream they live in, make the rules, and you and I either adapt our tactics accordingly or catch no fish.

One approach to stream tactics and their successful use is simple addition. Take all the major factors of the problem (catching the fish you want), add them together, and what you come up with should be the only logical way to go about the business of getting fish in the creel.

Say, for example, you want to catch stream salmon from Michigan's Betsie River. You know from experience that the river does in fact hold salmon at certain times of the year, so you make it your business to be on hand when the fish are present. That's the beginning of success—being there when the fish are.

You've been told the salmon hit best shortly after they enter the stream, so you fish only that section of the river within, say, 20 stream miles of the stream or river mouth, reasoning that any fish in that water probably has been there only a short time. That's step number two, and you're closer to success.

You do a bit of reading on the subject and learn that migrating salmon hit best when the water temperature is at or below 55°, and your trip is timed accordingly. That's step three.

Where on the stream can you gain access to the water, and what is the Betsie River like at those access points? Is the current fast and narrow? Are the pools deep? How much cover is present? Will you need medium or heavy tackle? Getting correct answers to the above will tell you a number of things, including whether you can wade or use a canoe or boat plus maybe an outboard, how much weight your line will need to reach fish level (6–8 feet on the Betsie), and maybe even what specific baits or lures you should use. You're almost home.

About all that remains is for you to get on the water, look over local conditions, and make that first cast. The "simple addition" method by no means guarantees success, but it sure as hell cuts down the odds of your ending up flailing the water with the wrong bait and tackle, perhaps when no salmon or bass or trout are present in the first place.

I'm not going to discuss here the habits of each stream species of fish—each is detailed at length elsewhere in this book—but I am going to touch on the major stream strategies

In-stream obstacles which block upstream movement by gamefish often create concentrations of fish immediately downstream, as this fisherman obviously is aware.

for the angler who is confronting new water for the first time and is somewhat unsure where to begin.

I always thought everyone knew before leaving home what type of fish were found in the water to be fished. Until, that is, I got a call from an angler who reads my newspaper column. I no longer believe all fishermen do pre-trip research, or even know what kinds of fish live in certain types of streams.

For years I had been writing about a certain limestone river in southwestern Ohio, discussing its smallmouth bass and panfish, its warm, murky waters, and so forth. Not once did I mention anything save bass and panfish from that stream.

Yet along came a phone call from a local chap who wanted to know where on the river he should fish to catch brown trout. I told him there were no trout of any kind, much less browns, anywhere in the river. He disagreed.

"My buddy fished up there yesterday and caught five big browns. I seen 'em," he explained, adding that his friend wouldn't tell him where the fish were caught. Quite obviously, *this* I had to see.

A day later the caller showed up with a color snapshot of his friend's "brown trout." The sharp, clear photo showed an obviously very happy angler holding up a quintet of the prettiest white suckers I'd seen in a long time. I bit my tongue, stifled a laugh, and congratulated his friend on the catch. I didn't have the heart to tell him they weren't what he thought they were.

Not long ago I fished a West Coast river for salmon. The day I arrived I had occasion to chat with the owner of a small resort located quite near a fish ladder on the river. He said the rains were late in coming and the river was low. Then he mentioned salmon, and my ears perked up.

"The water going over the ladder is pretty low, and those salmon I've seen trying to jump over haven't made it," he said. "Most of 'em try only once or twice, then they turn around and move back downstream. I think they must spawn between here and the ocean, because they aren't making it over the ladder."

What a break! Knowing this not only helped me avoid days of casting miles of river barren of fish, it told me the short stretch of river between the ocean and the fish ladder contained a concentration of salmon. That's where I spent my week, and had some of the hottest salmon fishing of my life. The fish ladder had been built to prevent upstream movement of the sea lamprey eel, but it might as well have been built for me personally, to make a normal fishing trip a memorable one. The difference came from knowing about it *before* I started to fish.

Michigan fisherman Stan Lievense, originator of the hot new "wiggle fly," carries a good supply on his fishing hat. This is a handy carrying spot—unless you lose the hat.

The same type of unusual concentration of gamefish exists in other situations. Stream smallmouth or trout will often migrate upstream to spawn, sometimes even entering small tributary waters in search of cool water and proper bedding material such as gravel or rock rubble. Drought, which dries up riffles and makes them impassable, can create natural barriers below which gamefish concentrate.

Many patterns of dry and wet flies are best fished directly upstream to obtain the most natural drift possible.

And never ever pass up a concentration of any kind of fish. Most gamefish and even panfish are predators which compete all their lives for the available food in a stream. Concentrations of fish heighten this competitiveness, and very often several fish can be caught from the same spot until their numbers are depleted. This can be as true for beaver-dam brook trout in Maine as it is for smallmouth bass in Arkansas or golden trout in the mountains of California.

Another way to tip the fish-catching odds in your favor on almost any stream and for any type of gamefish is to fish the rises. I'm not talking about casting to rising fish, but rather making sure you are on the water when the stream's water level is slowly coming up because of rainfall or snowmelt upstream. There is something about fresh water that rejuvenates fish, both resident species and those in the stream only to spawn. I have found this true time and time again.

Probably the most obvious example of this came about on a famous steelhead stream one October morning. The lower stream's water flow was determined by the timing and amount of water admitted through a hydroelectric plant and

Dropping the fly upstream, this flyfisherman watches his pattern drift down and across the feeding lane where most trout will be found.

dam upstream. At regular hours workers at the dam would sound an alarm siren marking the release of new water into the stream, and experienced steelheaders knew they could expect hot action until the new level stabilized. Some anglers became so dependent on the predictability of this, in fact, that they fished the river only at the predetermined hours.

I've found much the same to be true when fall drought has dropped salmon-stream levels drastically. Then sudden, heavy rainfall will bring river levels up a few inches, dropping water temperatures, which acts like a vacuum to pull schooling silver and king salmon from the river mouths into the streams. Wise is the angler who watches the effects of rainfall on his favorite stream. It very often pays.

Streamer flies, sometimes called bucktails, can be very effective when rain has raised local stream levels and added a little color to the water. Perhaps this is because gamefish become less wary in such temporarily murky conditions, or because baitfish—that part of the gamefish diet imitated by streamers—are more readily available and therefore being preyed upon more actively. Whatever the reason, do carry a

Learning the proper use of fishing tackle makes the sport far more enjoyable. Fishing clinics provide good instruction, and are fun to attend. The instructor here is Cortland's Leon Chandler, who has given clinics all over the world.

supply of white streamers, both weighted and unweighted. The streamer seems to be especially effective in locating and catching big stream trout and smallmouth bass when cast across and downstream, then permitted to hang directly downstream in the current while the rod tip twitches just enough to make the fly dart and fall back like a minnow battling the current. This method is especially effective when the fly is allowed to hang in the current in, around, and under streamside logjams, undercut banks, and other cover suspected to hold big fish. Most stream fish are predators by nature, and you'll sometimes get strikes on streamers hung in the current merely because you're making a tantalizing bait available to a big fish, even when that fish is not feeding.

Sometimes I think the streamer fly is almost irresistible to big gamefish. At least an experience I had on Victoria Island in Canada's Northwest Territories seems to bear this out.

I was in a party of anglers fishing for arctic char. The char—red-bellied males in their spawning scarlets and silver-sided females—were thick in the island's many tundra lakes and even in the short "rivers" draining one lake into another. David Kaomayok, my Inuit Eskimo guide, spied my fly rod and suggested we try flyfishing for char in a drainage river tumbling into the lake. We agreed and moved.

Although the flowing watercourse was only a few hundred yards long, there was plenty of white water above a broadening pool where the current slowly dissipated, and in this slick water we found dozens of slowly cruising char as they rose to sip tiny mosquito larvae from the surface. The larvae were quite small—the only dry-fly pattern in my book matching it was a tiny Adams tied on a No. 18 hook, and there was no way I could hope to turn, much less boat, one of these robust char on so small a barb.

David, my guide, looked over my fly selection a moment, then pulled a large white bucktail from the sheepskin. "You try this," he said, indicating my fly rod and the rising fish all around us.

I doubted if the char would suddenly abandon their top-water feeding to chase a fly designed to imitate a minnow, but I tied the streamer to a short, strong leader and dropped it several feet beyond the nearest rise. The bucktail had hardly moved a yard when the nearest char, easily seen in the clear water, suddenly changed course, swam directly after the fly, and engulfed it before turning away. I was so amazed I almost forgot to strike, but the char's momentum tightened the line and we were hooked up. I was even more surprised to see two other char chasing the first, apparently hopeful of stealing away his prize minnow. They too had abandoned their insect meal for the chance for a big mouthful of baitfish. That fish measured 35 inches long and weighed an even 15 pounds two hours later back at camp; it was my best char of the trip.

Marabou streamers, first cousins to the bucktail, can also be very effective. Wing fibers used to tie these flies are extremely supple in water and react to every bit of current and rod action. Marabous can be great fish-catchers in both shallow and deep water and can be tied with weighted bodies so they sink readily in heavy water. A friend and I were fishing Colorado's Roaring Fork River near Basalt shortly after a late snowfall had brought the stream level up several inches. The current was very fast with the new water, making mainstream fishing with fly tackle a real problem. But my compadre solved the problem by using a small white marabou streamer cast downstream and retrieved in a darting fashion past streamside cover. The rainbows loved it, and even a 15-inch brownie, hidden away from the roaring current under some shoreline boulders, nabbed the tantalizing marabou.

Stan Lievense, a good friend and fishing companion of mine from Michigan, has come up with an all-new fly designed for stream fish put off by the usual fare of dead-drift streamers and other no-action fly-rod baits. Until now, the only real action given flies was that imparted by the current or by the rod tip, but Lievense's invention promises to change all that.

Lievense reasoned that plugs have action, so why not flies. After much experimentation, his "wiggle fly" emerged. It features a plastic diving lip, a miniature of the plastic lip found on today's floating-diving plugs. The body is rather chubby and is dressed with the usual hair wing. Some models have tails and some do not. A line-attachment bracket, in the shape of a figure-8, is added to the hook eye to give the bait complete freedom of movement in the water.

Lievense's method of fishing his new fly is to cast it diagonally downstream, then either let it hang in the current or retrieve it very slowly against the current. Either method makes use of the plastic diving lip to impart a side-to-side wiggle to the bait. So far, Lievense has taken two kinds of salmon, steelhead, and domestic stream trout (rainbow and brown) on his invention.

"I've had people insist my wiggle fly is a lure, not a fly," Lievense says. "All I know is, it catches fish when other flies

Fish toward something. All stream fish gravitate toward available cover, and fishing such spots greatly increases your chances of success.

won't, and that's what I was shooting for." At last report, a West Coast tackle manufacturer was planning to market a commercial version of the wiggle fly, and I wouldn't be surprised if it becomes a favorite among West Coast trout and salmon fishermen.

I'm convinced there is one very important difference between strategies used for domestic stream fish—that is, those living there year-round—and anadromous species such as salmon (both Atlantic and Pacific) and steelhead, which enter moving water only to spawn.

The basic difference as far as the fish are concerned is the feeding urge, or the lack of it. Domestic trout, bass, panfish, and the rough species (carp and catfish) depend entirely on the stream and its habitat for food, shelter, and a place to spawn. As the stream's welfare goes, so go the domestic fish.

But the anadromous species enter rivers and streams only to spawn. Some reproduce and die (Pacific salmon), and some return again and again every year (steelhead, Atlantic salmon, and to a lesser extent, lake-run brown trout). None of these fish does a lot of feeding during the spawning run. They have stocked up on fat in the lake or ocean in preparation for the spawning migration and have little urge to feed when the river's current and tree-lined banks flank their shoulders. What little feeding these anadromous fish do is, I suspect, motivated more by their pure predatory nature and the competitive instinct aroused by their sheer numbers than by obedience to hunger.

All of which means that the basic fishing methods used for one of the two basic types of fish will, in all probability, be very different from those used for the other. It's simple: Domestic fish can be expected to feed regularly, while anadromous fish must be teased into striking, often by repeated presentation of the lure.

Here's an example. If you're after stream channel catfish and your bait is, say, a live minnow, you need only make the bait available to the fish to take it on that bait. If it is hungry and feeding, it will gobble the minnow the first time it comes near. If, however, you are fishing for steelhead, particularly in chilly spring waters when the steelies are still logy, you may have to drag that spinner or wobbling plug or spawn sac past your quarry's handsome gray snout a dozen times before it gets annoyed or excited enough to eat it. This is something of an oversimplification, I agree, but it *is* a good rule of thumb.

So is stream reading, defined for our purpose as determining where the species you seek will be located in each stream situation, and how to present your bait or lure to it in the best manner. Of course, this approach assumes the fisherman knows something about the fish he seeks before he ever loads his gear in the station wagon. You won't find bass in a Colorado snowmelt stream, nor is a coho salmon likely to show up in a tributary of the Mississippi River. Your personal experience, and the information contained in the species chapters in this book, should be sufficient background.

Let's say you're after stream crappie. It's mid-September, the weather has begun to cool, and water temperatures are down from their summer simmer. Stream waters are likely to be in pool or slightly below, and water clarity is good. Perhaps a few hardwood leaves have caught in the dead fin-

Lead sinker wire wrapped on the hook before starting the fly dressing will make the bait sink to fish level quickly and with less drift. Courtesy Dayton *Daily News.*

gers of half-submerged brushpiles and logs, clogging the stream known to contain crappie.

You already know that fall crappie congregate around brushpiles because such spots attract minnows, and the water must be fairly deep (say 4 feet minimum). You also know that crappie dislike heavy current, so you look for (1) wide, slow-moving pools, perhaps tucked away behind a sandbar or other natural barrier, plus (2) fairly deep water with (3) a good deal of submerged brush or other cover. Find these, and chances are you've located the crappie.

I cannot overemphasize the importance of not bumping or scraping crappie cover. Even the careless scraping or banging of metal objects in a boat can put crappie off their feed. If you are fishing from shore or wading, the chances of disturbing crappie cover is greatly lessened, of course, but stream crappie are often taken by boat fishermen or canoeists, and special care is required. Here's a tip: If the current threatens to move your boat away downstream from the brushpile, carefully tether your craft to the cover itself *on the downstream side*. This should hold your boat in one place and avoid constant adjustment of position. A brush anchor (see chapter on accessories) is a great aid here.

Here's another situation. Let's assume you're fishing for wary stream trout in a heavily fished stream. The pools are small, cover is minimal and the trout are so spooky they make the Abominable Snowman look like an extrovert. How will you fish?

The stream, if it's a typical trout river or brook, probably, for all its total width, has a relatively narrow constant current. This is the feeding lane, the natural conveyor belt which delivers drifted food to the fish. Regardless of how heavily fished the stream is, it's a good bet the trout will not be far from the lane. Finding the lane is easy. Riffles with a bit of white water usually develop a line of foam which traces the lane exactly. Lacking the foam, try crushing a dry leaf in your fingers and dropping the particles above the pool you want to fish. Then all you have to do is watch as the current moves the leaf particles through the pool; they will travel along the feeding lane.

If the water is fairly deep and the trout are relying on depth, rather than in-stream objects, for cover, you'll need to judge the current and decide how much weight is required to get your bait or lure to fish level. If it is the season of hatching insects, it could well be that the trout will come up for a drifted dry fly or lightly hooked natural insect, in which case all you need do is decide where to put it on the water to drift it over the fish, and from what direction to cast so you'll have enough slack line for a lifelike dead drift.

But perhaps the trout refuse to take a top-water bait. Then what? This requires a bit more use of the old bean. A natural bait of redworm or a single salmon egg may need a split shot or two to reach the deepest part of the pool while being shoved along by the current. A nymph or wet fly, of course, must be more carefully presented in order to appear natural. Quite a few dedicated nymphers cast directly upstream, mending line as the bait is carried toward them by the current. This allows the nymph to bounce and bump along bottom just as a real insect nymph would do, and a taking fish

Bob Daily fishes heavy cover because he knows trout prefer spots where they can remain hidden until food presents itself.

very often causes only a slight pause in this natural drift when it strikes. Wet flies are often fished diagonally upstream and allowed to swing down and past the angler like an emergent insect trying to reach the surface. So how you cast a fly to those wary stream trout depends on (1) where the fish are with respect to your position, (2) their depth, and (3) the type of fly you choose.

Today's market gives the angler quite a choice of fly lines. Each line is designed to handle specific flyfishing chores and can help create better anglers.

Level fly line has the same diameter and grain weight throughout. It is the workhorse fly line and is most popular among newcomers to the sport of flyfishing. It is also the least expensive.

Tapered fly lines are very popular today because their weight and bulk distribution aid in the proper presentation of the lures they are designed to cast. A weight-forward line, for example, has its greatest diameter and weight in the first third of its length, and since flycasting involves casting the *line* while the lure goes along for the ride, weight-forward lines do a better job of casting large or bulky flies, such as bass bugs and salmon streamers. Weight-forward lines carry the code prefix WF.

The double-taper line has its "belly" or greatest diameter in the middle of the line and usually allows the caster the greatest distance. Double-tapers have the added advantage of enabling the angler to reverse the line on his reel, front to back, when the old tip becomes worn. This is possible because both ends of the DT line are identical.

Besides their weight-distribution features, today's fly lines can be floating, sinking, or in between. Floating lines can, quite obviously, be used for fishing top-water baits such as dry flies, poppers, and bugs; they are also sometimes used to fish nymphs in shallow streams, and are used in combination with a specially designed sinking leader. The sinking line does just that—sinks by itself because of its density—and is often used on big, deep water with wet flies, big nymphs and the like. Full-sinking lines can be tough to pick up after a retrieve is completed, however, and may require a somewhat stouter rod than floating lines.

Big-river steelheaders, of course, need line specially designed to get down to fish level in heavy current. For this reason there are specialty lines such as high-density sinking lines with greater specific gravity, and a therefore greater rate of sink, than normal sinking line. Lead-core fly line is also available and is most popular on the West Coast, as is shooting-head line (see the chapter on steelhead).

Those who fish intermediate waters with streamers, or fairly shallow rivers with nymphs and wet flies, may choose a sinking-tip line. Only the first 10 feet or so of the 30-yard line sinks; the remainder floats just like a full floating model.

Cortland has come out with an interesting line especially for those flyfishermen who fish nymphs. Called a Nymph-Tip, the line is full-floating and the first 6 inches of its working tip are colored a bright fluorescent red. The red tip acts like a bait fisherman's float, relaying the slight touch of a fish taking a nymph.

Fly-line codes have changed for the better over the years as well. They are now much simpler and more easily read, and are in three basic parts. Take the line code WF-7-F. The WF means the line is weight-forward, the 7 refers to the line's overall grain weight, which is matched to the rod, and the F means it is a floating line. DT-5-S means a double-taper sinking line, while L-5-ST means a level sinking-tip line; in both cases the 5 indicates the grain weight, as shown in the table below. The number system, by the way, is standardized by the American Fishing Tackle Manufacturers Association of Chicago, and makes correctly matching line to rod a snap.

AFTMA FLY LINE STANDARDS

Line No.	Weight in Grains	Tolerance
1	60	54–66
2	80	74–86
3	100	94–106
4	120	114–126
5	140	134–146
6	160	152–168
7	185	177–193
8	210	202–218
9	240	230–250
10	280	270–290
11	330	318–342
12	380	368–392

Here's a tip for the chap in the market for his first flyfishing outfit of rod, reel, and line. The key is *balance,* and it starts with knowing a couple of things about what you want to do. If you know you'll be fishing for small-stream trout and bass with the new fly rig, it follows you'll know what type of lures you'll be using. As I've explained, certain fly lines, or types of fly lines, are more suited to casting nymphs or dry flies or poppers than others, so start by knowing the lure types you'll use, then choose a line to do the job. The rest is all downhill.

Once you have line in hand, match the grain weight of the line (indicated by the number) to the rod you are considering.

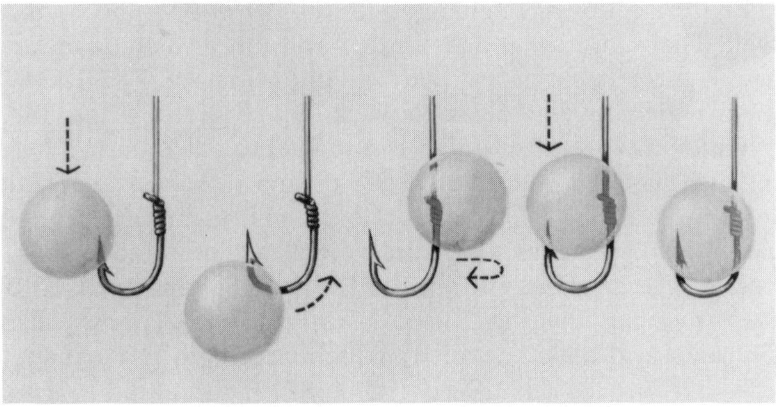

Baits of single salmon eggs can be excellent for steelhead, stream trout, and even salmon. Here's the correct way to hook single eggs. It both hides the hook and provides a firm hold for the fragile-skinned egg. Courtesy Uncle Josh Bait Co.

Rods meant to cast dry flies have soft tips, while big-water rods are rather stout, with a lot of muscle. Better yet, take along a friend who flyfishes successfully and let him or her help you choose, along with the tackle dealer.

OK, now all you need is a reel. I vote for either the single-action or multiplying type. Why? Because they have far fewer parts to wear out, and because spring-loaded automatic fly reels have a way of freezing up when that big whopper gets the current behind him and takes off for New Jersey. Single-action reels produce one turn of the line spool for every manual turn of the handle, while multiplying reels contain gearing which increases the number of spool revolutions for each turn of the handle. The latter is popular on big, wide rivers.

Whatever reel you choose, however, it is used mainly as a place to store line, though when equipped with a drag it can be used as an aid in slowing the runs of big fish. The reel's overall weight helps balance the whole outfit for tireless casting too.

But whatever species of stream fish you're after, I'd suggest you use the lightest tackle capable of doing the job. This goes for all kinds of tackle, not just fly tackle. Light, small-diameter line will not spook as many fish as heavy line, and it casts farther on spinning, spincasting, and baitcasting gear while

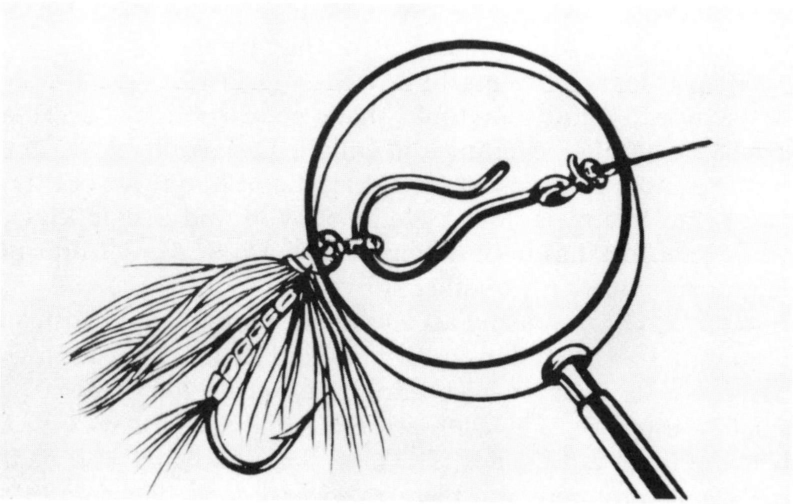

Many types of wet flies are best fished with maximum freedom of movement during the drift. Mustad's special fly attachment provides the needed movement. Courtesy O. Mustad and Sons.

permitting lighter lures to be used. And the lighter your gear, the less disturbance it causes on the water, always important in shallow-water situations. My two young daughters are just learning to fish with the two-piece cane poles I bought them, yet each pole is equipped with 6-pound-test monofilament line. The girls have learned that this tackle won't stand abuse; even palm-sized bluegills have to be landed with care. Neither girl has happened onto a real lunker yet, but when they do I'll bet my best fly rod they'll not lose it because of broken line.

A group of Michigan steelheaders have come up with a very unusual tackle combination for their sport. They put 2-pound-test monofilament on fly rods and fish single salmon eggs in their many steelhead rivers each spring and fall. And they catch fish—on 2-pound-test line, mind you. I suspect they don't defeat many steelhead. They probably just discuss matters with the fish and finally *encourage* them to surrender.

Stream-fishing tactics are, I believe, a combination of impersonal stream conditions—water temperature, clarity, gradient, and the transient or resident fish species—plus the personal end of things, such as the angler's choice of tackle and how he prefers to fish it. How these two groups of variables mesh determines the success of the day astream.

When things aren't meshing well, you just have to do the best you can—and sometimes that's good enough. I recall a lovely September evening on Ohio's East Fork Creek, the southernmost tributary of the Little Miami River. An oddity: The Little Miami is now a National Wild and Scenic River, while East Fork has been dammed by the U.S. Army Corps of Engineers. But that's another story.

In any event, I was on East Fork that evening armed with an ultralight spinning rod and a pouchful of light balsa plugs designed to float at rest and dive when retrieved. The smallmouth bass, however, were having a field day with a hatch of large caddis flies. The long slick of water I was wading was frothy here and there as several good bass tore into the plentiful floating insects, and there I was with no fly rod.

Then I tried something. I cast the small, light plug as far upstream as I could, letting it float back down with only slight rod twitches to impart a little life. That's not the way a plug "should" be fished, and it certainly was crude as a caddis imitation. But the unsophisticated smallmouth loved it. Before full dark descended on that now-flooded little woodland stream I'd caught ten decent bass, releasing all but two destined for a frying pan.

So maybe stream tactics, after all, are really nothing more than doing the best you can with what you've got—tackle, stream conditions, and a little imagination.

LIVE BAIT IN STREAMS

I've seen it happen time and again. A handful of dedicated fly-rod purists seeking trout flail their favorite stream for an entire day, yet when the last finely wadered leg has departed the stream, only a few 6-inch trout have come to hand, 10X leader points and a dozen fly patterns notwithstanding. Then along comes a chap, no less dedicated to catching trout (or bass or panfish or whatever) but willing to use live baits matching those natural foods found in the stream, who no sooner puts worm to water when a lunker fish gobbles the gob, putting him immediately ahead of the departed flyfishermen. It happens all the time, and I for one think it's hilarious.

Here are a bunch of squinty-eyed purists arguing over whether their favorite pattern of nymph or dry fly should contain twenty-four hairs in its hackle or twenty-two hairs, and while all this is going on a chap shows up who doesn't know hackles from horseshoes, and he catches all the fish. And that, as we used to say in the Air Force, is a real honk.

One flyfishermen's club I know of makes it a point in each monthly newsletter to proclaim the club's goal of stamping out all use of the dreaded earthworm for trout. Members scheme for it, gloat over it, plan for it, and may even pray for it. Why? I suspect, when all is said and done, it's because the earthworm all too often catches the most trout and the largest trout, while in the bargain requiring far less effort on the fisherman's part. That is not the kind of track record a fly-rod snob can go up against and expect to come out on the winning end.

Show me a trout or smallmouth bass or spotted bass or crappie that won't hit a drifted nightcrawler in murky water before he'll take an artificial, and I'll show you an exception. Fish for smallmouth bass in deep pools, particularly in early spring or the dog days of summer, and I'll show you a fish that will reject all manner of lures, but smack a large minnow or worm with gusto.

Put the facts on the table: There are times when live bait has it all over artificials. And there are fishermen—legions of them—all over this country who would *rather* fish with bait than with artificial lures. Sure, there are snobs who will insist such folks are not playing the game fairly, but who cares? Live and let fish, right?

Tell you what. You and me'll use whatever catch fish, while the snobs use excuses, OK?

EARTHWORMS

I've put worms first in this chapter because they are far and away the most widely used and consistently effective live bait of the lot. Under one condition or another they will catch every type of freshwater fish in North America save members of the pike family, are very easy to gather and store, and are darned hard to fish incorrectly. That's as close to a surefire fish catcher as I can recommend.

The nightcrawler, also called dew worm because of its habit of venturing out of its burrow in the dewy night, is probably the most commonly used live bait. Day in and day out, more 'crawlers are gathered by fishermen, sold by bait dealers, and gobbled by sport fish than all other live baits combined. Fish which have never before seen a worm (and this surely in-

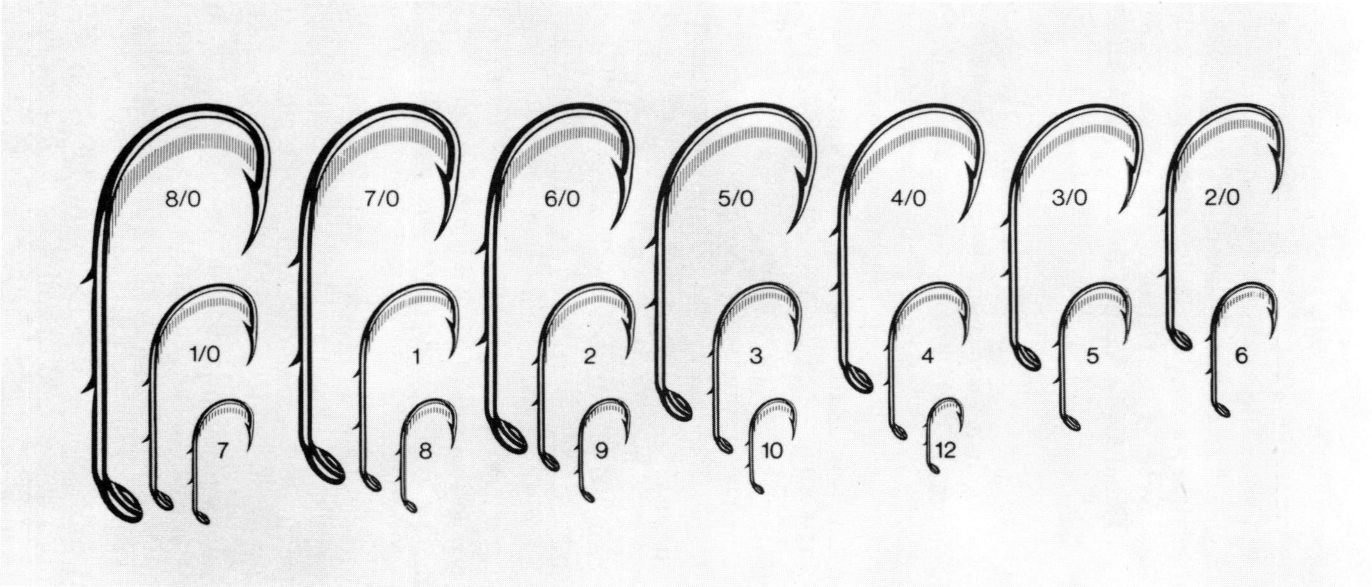

Hooks used for live bait must be designed for firm hooking, strength, and the ability to keep the bait on the hook during casting. This selection of Mustad Beak hooks with the sliced (barbed) shank will do the job. Courtesy O. Mustad and Sons.

cludes almost all of them) will charge up and eat a worm with no hesitation. Perhaps there is something about the nightcrawler's scent in the water, the way it writhes and wiggles on a hook, its overall generous size, which attracts so many species of gamefish. I admit I don't know the answer.

I recall visiting a very exclusive and private trout-fishing club tucked away in the wooded hills of New England. The club grounds held a real jewel of a trout pond fed by pure artesian well water, and trout could be seen swimming around 20 feet below the surface. The club's caretaker insisted that any fishing a friend and I did comply with club rules—flies only. We fished for an hour or so with no strikes and only passing interest in our varied patterns by the supersophisticated rainbows and brookies. Finally, with the caretaker out of sight and secure in the opinion that we weren't *really* breaking the rules, we turned over a large stone, located a small nightcrawler, and tossed it, free of any hook or line, into the pond.

The worm was immediately charged by at least a dozen of the big trout. The lucky one grabbed it and darted away, closely pursued by half a dozen others trying to steal the prize. I have no doubt that none of those trout had so much as seen a worm before, yet each was anxious to gobble it with no hesitation. Sure, it may have resembled the food pellets tossed on the water by the caretaker every evening, but once in the water the worm took on its true form to the trout: long, wiggly, and not at all like a food pellet.

Fishing the nightcrawler in rivers and streams puts two good things together: the natural movement of the bait in the current, and the natural movement of the bait itself. Fish such as smallmouth bass and large trout seem to react best to a 'crawler hooked just once, through the worm's collar (that dark band in its body a few inches behind its head). This hooking method permits the worm to coil, writhe, and wiggle and often attracts the largest fish that sees it because the bait is simply irresistible. Single-hooking is best done with a light, short-shank hook for the best possible drift, and this necessitates careful casting so as not to throw the worm off the hook. I like to use a soft-tipped spinning or fly rod for this purpose;

the soft rod tip is easier on the bait while allowing good casting distance and accuracy.

The 'crawler's pliable body lends itself to drift-fishing through riffles and slicks of fast, flat water. In fact this can be one of the deadliest of all presentations, because natural earthworms are often obtained by the fish in just this manner. In spring, for example, heavy rainfall dislodges worms from shoreline soil and washes them into the current. The creatures have no defense against the push of the current and simply drift along with the river, sweeping around rocks and through riffles and wiggling tantalizingly inches off bottom in the pools below. Fish are used to seeing worms in this manner, so imitating the approach is making the best of a good thing. Using this drift method I've caught smallmouth, trout, channel and blue catfish, rock bass, spotted bass, and even a few carp. When the river is up from recent rains and perhaps a bit murky, many kinds of fish move to the heads of pools, expectantly awaiting the increased food supply the river will deliver. Add a higher level of dissolved oxygen at such spots in midsummer and you have an unbeatable fishing location.

Nightcrawlers do just that—they crawl at night. A drizzling shower or long spate of lawn sprinkling will bring the worms aboveground along about ten p.m.; trying to gather worms much sooner than that often fails because the creatures take quite some time to come completely out of their burrows, and grabbing just the front end while the rear remains anchored belowground often results in only half a worm.

I use a simple two-cell flashlight with red or yellow cellophane over the face. The cellophane reduces the glare of the light and doesn't alert the wary nightcrawlers, which have light-sensitive nerves along their body. It's also important to tread as lightly as possible, because the worms can detect the vibrations of a heavy footfall and will zip underground quickly. Sometimes I wear tennis shoes if the worms are particularly touchy. You may also want to study an exposed worm for a second or two, just long enough to decide which end is the head and which is the tail. Grab the *tail* first, if you can, because the 'crawler always dives tail-first for cover when threatened.

Some lawns are always better than others for gathering nightcrawlers. A regular program of watering and fertilization assures a steady supply of nightcrawlers. I recall the grassy lawn surrounding an old concrete water tower in the community where I grew up. The tower was old and leaked water, keeping the surrounding lawn moist all summer long. This was a consistently good place to gather nightcrawlers, rain or no rain. Another good spot is a golf course.

Nightcrawlers are easily stored. You can obtain an old washtub and fill it with dry leaves. Moisten the leaves a bit every week, just enough to make the leaves lightly matted without overwetting them. This setup will support many dozens of worms which eat the leaves and enrich the bed with their excretions. Just be sure to examine the tub closely every few days for dead worms, which should be removed and discarded immediately. Store the tub in a cool, moist spot away from chemicals and strong odors.

Some anglers and almost all bait-store dealers use old refrigerators for storing worms. An upright model can be stored in the back of a garage or a basement corner and will keep 1,000 or more 'crawlers fresh and healthy. Temperature inside the unit should be somewhere between 45° and 55°. The worms can be stored in several Styrofoam trays. Probably the best are trays measuring about 6 inches high by 15 inches long by 15 inches wide. Worm-food bedding, sphagnum moss, or other worm-bedding material should be placed in the tray to a level of 4 inches, and it's a good idea to cut small holes in each side below the level of the bedding and cover them with fine-mesh screening, allowing for air circulation. Up to 300 adult nightcrawlers can be stored in such a tray, and the refrigerator will hold several such trays, enough for an entire season's fishing.

The same storage method works for the smaller earthworms, known as garden worms, redworms, angleworms, etc. These are about one-half to one-third the size of nightcrawlers and fill the need for a smaller but lively bait for stream trout, panfish, and the occasional fussy smallmouth which refuses a large bait. Redworms too are best fished on light hooks, but the prescription often calls for more

Examination of the tiny creatures in a stream enables fishermen to offer the fish his usual diet, improving their chances for success. A small dipnet and sharp eye are all that is required.

than one worm on the hook, creating the large, wiggling gob so effective for bullheads, channel catfish, the odd carp, and other sizable fish.

Panfish, like no other species in my experience, are great bait-stealers. No sooner is a freshly baited hook dropped in the water than the bait's been nibbled off and another must be added. But there is an answer. Simply run the point of the hook into the worm's head, continuing until the entire worm is impaled. This makes it almost impossible for a larcenous fish to get the worm without also taking the hook, and it hides the telltale hook at the same time. This method is especially effective on bluegills, sunfish, and crappies.

If ten minutes of shovel labor isn't your idea of fun, here's an easy method of getting worms out of the ground. Someone you know may gather walnuts in the fall. If so, ask him to save all the walnut hulls for you, then place the green hulls in a tub of cold water and let the mixture brew for a few days, until the water has been stained a dark brown. Once the mixture is ready, select a spot known to contain worms and pour the mixture generously directly on the spot. The walnuty water will seep into the ground and give the worms it reaches a mild burn, sending them scurrying to the top like Polaris missiles. Then all you need do is gather them and rinse them briefly in clean water, and you've got fish bait without shovel labor.

CRAYFISH

Many professional river guides I know rate the lowly little crayfish as *the* top bait for big-river smallmouth bass. Fished whole (with or without pincers), crayfish drifted weightless through deep pools and past bassy-looking boulders have accounted for more sizable smallmouth than any other attraction, live or artificial. I think this is true simply because stream bass, not to mention lunker stream trout, channel cats, and the infrequent carp, depend so heavily on this plentiful crustacean found in nearly every state and province.

Crayfish, sometimes called craws, crawdads, freshwater lobsters, and so on, have no internal skeleton and rely on their outer shell (exoskeleton) for protection. Fish pursue and eat hardshelled crayfish at any time of the year, but seem to have a special appetite for softshell crayfish, actually a misnomer because the "softshell" crayfish has no shell at all during its

Crayfish, considered by many to be the best bait for large smallmouth bass, are best hooked whole by impaling the tail from the underside. Hook then rides upright and avoids snags.

molting period, which occurs several times a summer to accommodate body growth.

After much observation I've come to believe that stream fish prefer softshell crayfish simply because they are far less mobile and are found in shallow water, and therefore are easier to catch than hardshell crayfish. When molting time comes, the creature crawls into the stream shallows where the current is slack, sheds its old shell, and patiently awaits the formation of a new, larger shell before scuttling back to deep water and a rock to crawl under. During this brief period, the crayfish is especially vulnerable to attack by prowling gamefish.

If the whole crayfish, hardshell or softshell, is to be fished, the hooking method most often seen is once through the base of the tail. I like to insert the hook point underneath the tail, running it completely through the tail and out to top layer of shell, exposing all of the hook plus the barb. This hooking method lets me scuttle and hop the crayfish on retrieve while keeping the bait and hook snag-free. Big-river fishermen seeking monster flathead and blue catfish often use a treble hook where legal, but still use only one of the three hooks to secure the crayfish to the line.

Stream catfish and even large trout are often suckers for crayfish tails fished dead on bottom. The tail breaks off easily where it joins the body and can be strung on a large hook much like a redworm bait. Again, I think it important to expose the point and hook barb for solid hookups on the strike. Crayfish tails are for some reason especially effective when dead-line fished on bottom at night. Maybe this is because the truly large fish which prefer this bait are most active after dark.

Crayfish to be stored until the next fishing trip will remain healthy if kept in the same refrigerator used for worms, and in identical Styrofoam trays. Place as many crayfish in the tray as are needed to cover the bottom, then cover them with a damp cloth and place them in the refrigerator. The cool temperature will keep the craws fresh and slow their metabolism enough so that no feeding is necessary provided they are stored for only a week or so. Softshell craws will keep in the same manner without forming new hard shells. If craws are to be kept longer than a week or ten days, it's a good idea to freeze them in convenient amounts and thaw them thoroughly just before departing for the trip. They will appear fresh and will catch a lot of bottom-feeding fish.

HELLGRAMMITES

The hellgrammite, the larval stage of the dobsonfly, is found in many warm-water streams in North America where pollution is either not present or is kept to a minimum. These coal-black, flat-bodied creatures have many sets of legs, a hardshell collar just behind the head, a pair of muscular pincers capable of drawing blood, and a pair of clinging legs at the tail used to cling to the undersides of submerged stream rocks. In streams where they exist, live hellgrammites can be the very best bait for several types of gamefish, including smallmouth and spotted bass, channel cats, flatheads, rock bass, and green sunfish. Hellgrammites are tough-bodied little creatures reaching lengths up to 5 inches overall. They seem to stay forever on a hook and are therefore excellent for drift-fishing, not to mention attracting and catching several fish per bait.

The easiest way to capture hellgrammites, and to avoid getting pinched in the process, is to join forces with another angler. One angler stretches a mesh minnow or bait seine across a particularly rocky, swift-moving section of the stream, making sure the leading (upstream) edge of the seine is dead on bottom. The other chap then moves a few feet directly upstream from the seine and uses his hands or feet to turn over and otherwise disturb all the rocks in the vicinity. Hellgrammites, when dislodged from their hiding places under rocks, immediately roll into a ball and drift downstream with the current. It's amazing how many of these ferocious little creatures can be gathered in half an hour or so on streams where they are plentiful. I've found, however, that eight or ten are usually enough for a full day's fishing, because they stay on the hook so well.

Hellgrammites can be fished with or without a float or bobber, depending on the gamefish you're after. Channel cats often prefer their food to drift along near but not touching bottom, and for this a light float is called for, while smallmouth bass, which regularly feed on hellgrammites, expect the bait to be bouncing along in the current, skipping over every rock and dropping between every cluster of bottom cover. For bass, then, I like to use a light spinning rod or fly outfit, no more than one split shot for casting weight, and a short-shank No. 10 or No. 12 wire hook. This rig is cast into a riffle and allowed to drift naturally into the head of the pool. When the line stops or twitches, the bait has been grabbed, but don't strike immediately. Bass and other gamefish have a habit of merely grasping part of the hellgrammite in their lips while they swim off a few feet before accepting the entire bait—and your hook—into their mouths. When that second run starts, tighten up and cross his eyes.

Hellgrammites can be stored for a few days in a shallow tub containing an inch or so of water and enough rocks above the water level to give the creatures room to haul out. If the bait is to be transported before it's used for bait, use a coffee can containing damp newspaper or leaves.

The hellgrammite's tough collar provides a handy place to place the hook. Start from beneath the neck and bring the hook point right through the collar. This may kill the bait, but no matter; stream fish take the helgy dead as well as alive.

You aren't going to believe this, but it's true. I once had a freshly hooked hellgrammite do the catching for me. I was fishing a small Midwestern creek for smallmouth and had baited with a large hellgrammite. Apparently a very small rock bass came by to investigate the helgy's plight, because when the line twitched and I struck, I found a very surprised rock bass, no longer than my thumb, clamped firmly by the lower lip by a very irate hellgrammite. The creature's pincers held long enough for me to bring the little fish to hand. This should give some indication of just how tenaciously a hellgrammite's pincers can pinch.

CRICKETS AND HOPPERS

Picture this: It's a warm morning in May and the meadow stream you plan to fish is glassy-smooth beneath its bank cover of overhanging grass and weeds. No fish are to be seen, but past experience tells you the fish take refuge from the sun beneath the tufts of grass along the bank. A few minutes' searching in the nearby fields produces half a dozen active little green grasshoppers, and from beneath a rotting log you pull a few soft-bodied black crickets. These bugs, added to your light fishing tackle, are just the ticket for sun-shy bass or trout.

A single hopper is impaled on a light wire hook tied to a light leader. The bait ready, you approach the stream carefully, stopping a few feet from the bank and extending your rod over the water. The bait is slowly lowered to the surface,

Some creeks can contain surprisingly plentiful live bait. All that's needed is a seine. Be sure to check state laws on bait collecting first.

and although you can't see it, you know the hopper is either resting on the surface, where its kicking sends out telltale ripples, or is just under the surface, where it's easily seen by any fish hiding in the grass.

This is the classic way to fish crickets and grasshoppers. Stream fish living near grassy fields make a summer career of gobbling these fat little creatures, often patrolling the grassy banks in search of any bug luckless enough to tumble into the lion's den. The secret is to use *live* crickets or hoppers on hooks *light* enough to permit a natural presentation. I've had super days for big brown trout too sophisticated for flies but positively eager for a mouthful of live bait.

Here's a neat way to keep captured crickets and hoppers from jumping out of the bait container as soon as you put them in. Beg, borrow, or steal an old nylon stocking from your wife (or maybe from under the rear seat of your teenage son's jalopy) and wad it into the bottom of your hopper can. Grasshoppers and crickets have legs covered with tiny barbs for better traction, and these barbs become entangled in the nylon mesh, anchoring the bugs in their container until you remove them one by one.

Grasshoppers, almost impossible to catch when the sun is high, are easily grabbed if the fisherman will do his searching in the early morning when the field is still cool and dewy. Grasshoppers need the heat of the sun to warm them for the day's activities, and it's an easy matter to capture all you want before the dew disappears, when the creatures find it difficult to move.

THE PANFISH KILLERS

There are two highly effective live baits for panfish which we seldom see mention of in print but often see astream. I don't know their proper scientific names (this fact has yet to bother a fish), but they are commonly known as waxworms and mousies.

The waxworm is the larva of a small moth which deposits her eggs (rather brave of her, really) in active beehives. The eggs hatch into half-inch white wormlike creatures which

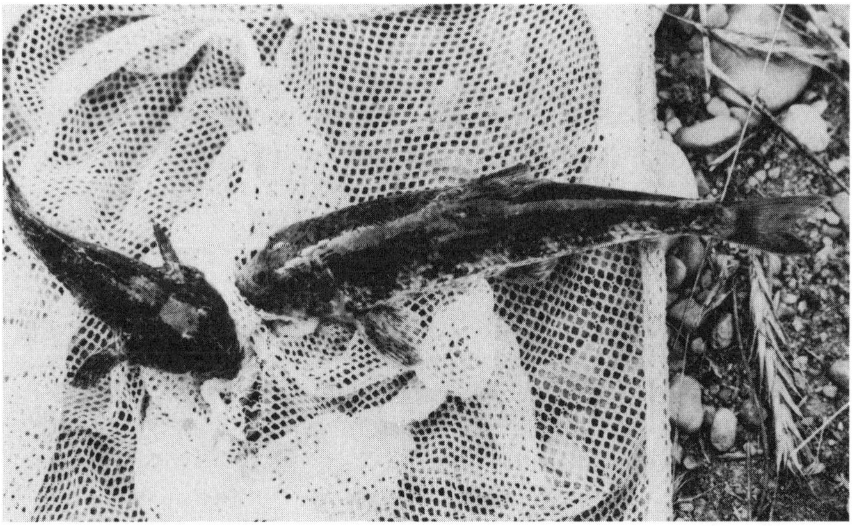

A sculpin (left) and a hog-nosed sucker, both major food items for trout of 3 pounds or more, are easily imitated with large streamer flies. Bait fishermen can capture and use the actual fish for bait.

feed on the hive's wax. Waxworms can be stored for several weeks in dry sawdust-filled containers with holes punched in the lid. They make very good bait for bluegills and crappies when fished one or two at a time on a tiny wire hook. Waxworms are soft-bodied and must be handled with care, but they make excellent winter bluegill bait when nothing else seems to work.

Mousies are fruitfly larvae. They are called mousies because they look like miniature mice. They are rather fuzzy, less than an inch long, and gray in color, appearance, and (I kid you not) they have a mouselike tail about as long as the body. Here's an easy way to gather them. Any canning plant discharges fruit offal, among it leftover pulp and skins of tomatoes, and this is the material the adult fruitfly chooses for her eggs. It can be sort of messy, digging through half-rotted piles of fruit leftovers, but you should soon locate a ball of hundreds of these little gray worms which are death on panfish of all kinds.

Apparently mousies seek both seclusion and security, because 18-inch strips of corrugated cardboard placed in a container holding mousies will soon be filled with them, one mousie to every little cavity in the corrugation. The strip is then rolled up and taken along, providing its own bait container. Try one or two of these odd little larvae on a No. 10 gold hook the next time you fish for panfish. They can fill a stringer quickly.

MINNOWS

Fishing guides and successful baitfishermen tell me minnows are such good bait because so many truly large predatory gamefish depend on smaller fish for the bulk of their diet. This sounds good to me, and the results of a lifelong angler addiction bears it out.

Minnows always, or nearly always, produce, whether in stream, river, pond, or lake. They are easily transported to the water, they provide their own action when alive, and they keep producing after death when large catfish or trout are around.

The term "minnow" is a catchall. Few are the anglers who specify which type of minnows they want, as long as they are of the right size and appear to be healthy. Some use shad fry, others like the emerald shiner, still others use small suckers, and some specify only "lake minnows" as opposed to "stream minnows," whatever *that* means. Generally speaking, crappies and other panfish are sought with minnows between 1 and 3 inches in length, while large trout, bass, and catfish are enticed with minnows from 3 to 10 inches long. The larger the minnow, however, the fewer may be kept alive in a small container.

There are two schools of thought about how to hook a minnow. One has it that the little fish should be hooked once, and then only through the back just ahead of or behind the dorsal, being careful not to injure the spine. The other folks swear minnows are best hooked through both lips, being careful not to touch the brain. Both methods allow the minnow to remain alive on the hook, and this is important because of the little fish's natural swimming movements. And some anglers say it's best to clip one or two of the minnow's fins to make the

Minnows hooked through both lips will live longer and remain more active if the brain is not damaged in hooking.

minnow appear injured in the water and therefore an easier mark for a hungry fish. I have never found this necessary, however.

When wading or fishing from a shallow-draft boat, I like to fish a live minnow on light line and a long rod directly beside sunken fish cover, such as fallen logs, stumps, etc. Any fish hiding there is fair game for this method.

When this method produces nothing, I put a minnow below a small bobber and cast it directly into the current. This is a game of cat and mouse as the fish takes the minnow, bobs the bobber, and the fight is on. Most gamefish take all of the minnow right now, with no preliminaries.

Catfishermen use minnows in a couple of ways, both effective. Live minnows are fished 18 inches below a float in the current for channel cats. And dead minnows, sometimes with strips of skin cut so they hang from the carcass, are placed in the sun and allowed to ripen a bit. The entire bait is then

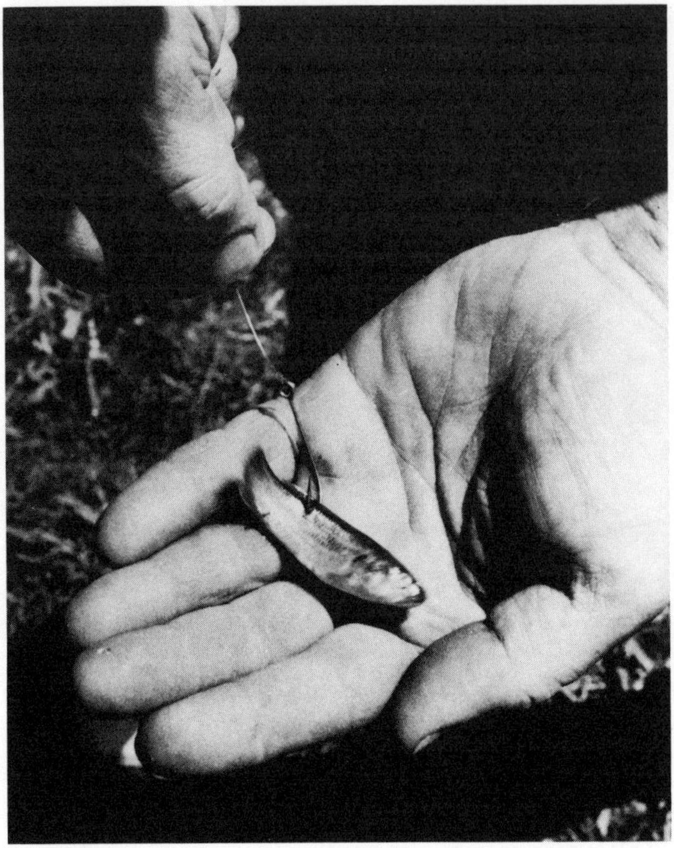

Minnows hooked just ahead or behind the dorsal fin, avoiding the spine, should remain lively. This minnow flipped to prove it just as the camera clicked.

strung on a large hook and cast on bottom in the stream's deepest pools. This is especially effective at night when the big cats prowl.

Minnow traps, nets, and seines are all employed to capture live minnows, but one word of caution: Do take the time to check with your state's conservation department before catching your own minnows. A tributary of an Ohio trout stream contains a very rare little fish called the tongue-tied chub, and bait taking is prohibited in the creek because of the chub's limited habitat. States sometimes designate bait-taking waters, how the minnows may be captured, and how many may be kept at any one time. Check and be sure.

STREAM PANFISH

Panfish, it seems to me, serve the same noble purpose in streams and small rivers they do in ponds and lakes. The game and plentiful little fish seem always willing to hit a bait or lure, and are easy enough to catch for even the most fidgety child just learning to handle a cane pole.

What panfish lack in size is more than compensated for by their sheer numbers. Show me the kid with a new fishing rig, or an adult with a light fly rod or spincasting rig, and I'll show you a fisherman equipped to make the most of the eight major panfish species found in this continent's warmwater streams and rivers.

BLUEGILL

The bluegill *(Lepomis machrochirus),* easily the top dog among panfishermen frequenting lakes and ponds, is also present in a great many streams all across the country, where it is sometimes called copperbelly, bream, blue, 'gill, and other nicknames fostered out of familiarity and fondness. In fact, so familiar is this game little slabside, it's more than even money that most of today's truly accomplished anglers served apprenticeships catching bluegills before graduating to salmon or bass or whatever. Bluegills are widespread, easy to catch, pugnacious fighters, and more than hold their own on the dinner table.

The bluegill, with some local variation due to water clarity and diet, is colored olive on the back, lightening to six to eight vertical black bars on the sides, and fading into dull cream on the belly. The broad gill flap bears a blue-black spot on its rearmost edge, from which comes the fish's name. Fins are creamy white to yellow, and the pectoral fin is distinctly pointed.

Stream bluegills, as do most other panfish found in moving water, prefer the large, slow-moving pools, especially those with plenty of weeds, stumps, fallen logs, and other rather dense cover. Young bluegills remain in cover during the day, while the adults, which in streams rarely exceed 10–12 inches in length, prefer to remain in open water during the day, moving to shoreline cover in early morning and late evening, when the best fishing occurs.

Young bluegills depend on aquatic insects and their nymphs (larvae) and plankton for their diet. As the fish mature, however, bluegills eat crayfish, all types of insects, and small baitfish, the fry of other panfish, and various forms of vegetation.

Nearly all stream panfish, including bluegills, definitely prefer a slow-moving artificial bait rather than one cranked back to the boat at bass-fishing speed. Bluegills will very often want to inspect a bait or lure closely before deciding to strike, and a slow retrieve with some stops and starts included gives them the opportunity to look over your offering. This is especially true when fishing dry flies, rubber spiders, poppers, and other floating baits. It's often possible to watch a bluegill attracted to your bait follow it back to the boat, darting in and then retreating as if unable to make up its mind. When the fish finally pulls the trigger, however, the strike is seldom dramatic. The bluegill merely charges the floating bait, sucks it in, and darts away, often pursued by other bluegills trying to wrestle the bait from its mouth. The strike on top-water baits and lures is usually accompanied by the identifiable and definitely audible slurp or pop created by the fish's sucking movements.

I have caught stream bluegills while fishing for smallmouth bass with tiny spinners and diving plugs, but such lures require a retrieve usually too rapid for the bluegill's liking.

Harold Barefoot, a good friend with something of a reputation hereabouts as a stream fisherman, waits until the first week in October to fish for bluegills. He claims only then are the fish sufficiently concentrated for good fishing on live bait, but admits the same time of year brings a mat of dead leaves to his favorite bass streams, making the casting of plugs for bass wellnigh impossible, so he switches over to bait and blues. The tactic has remained productive until as late as the first week in December in the Midwest, perhaps even later in the South.

Wherever the bluegill is found, it is in plenty. The species has the reputation of a prolific breeder, and rightly so. For this reason the larger pools of streams holding blues can and do become overpopulated with the game panfish, with the direct result being too many fish for the available food supply. This causes stunted bluegills, and often fully mature adults will measure no more than 6 inches. This situation provides a great opportunity to introduce youngsters to the pleasures of stream fishing. Bait their hooks with redworms, crickets, or waxworms, sit them down beside a half-submerged brushpile, and tell them to fish as close to the brush as possible, then stand back and watch. If bluegills are present, they should soon be coming ashore as quickly as the bait hits the water. So what if the fish are small? So are the kids.

Be sure to keep all the fish you catch, no matter how small, as this reduces pressure on food supplies and provides excellent garden fertilizer and good tablefare. Here's an easy and very tasty recipe for preparing bluegill fillets, using even the smallest fish. Thoroughly mix one cup pancake mix, one egg, one teaspoon salt, and one cup beer. Dip fillets in batter, drain excess, and dip fillets individually into hot (360°) fat. Fry to golden brown, drain on paper toweling, and serve with tartar sauce and lemon. Bill Gressard of Kent, Ohio, served

Patience is not a trait native to the young, but this little girl, the author's daughter Jenny, seems content to wait for a bluegill to bite.

this to me several years ago and I've never tasted bluegills prepared any better.

Blues will hit a fairly wide variety of slow-moving baits, provided they are small enough for the fish's rather small mouth. Trout-sized dry flies are good, especially in later summer near weedbeds, and so is an ingenious spoonlike fly-rod bait made from the circular bottom portion of a beer can. Use metal shears to cut the soft aluminum can bottom into circles slightly smaller in diameter than a dime. Then align a wire hook across the disc you've created, carefully folding the aluminum in half over the hook shaft. The hook point should be positioned on the folded side of the aluminum so that the point roughly parallels the straightedge. This lure is quite light and easily handled on a fly rod as is, or you can add a daub of paint on each side of the lure to simulate eyes. The aluminum's soft gray color resembles the bluegill's own fry, on which it feeds ravenously, and the bait is light enough so that it can be retrieved very slowly at whatever depth is called for.

The standard fly-rod baits for bluegills—spiders, bugs, cork poppers, wet flies—also take stream bluegills if fished slowly.

Little fish, big smile. Panfish are perfect for introducing children to the sport of fishing. Here Kelly Bowring, age eight, is obviously happy with her worm-caught trophy.

CRAPPIE

The crappie, perhaps the best-known schooling fish in lakes and ponds, is caught there in the early spring and again in late fall, when the silver-sided fish concentrate themselves near available food sources, in most cases large clouds of minnows. The same is true in streams, yet most fishing for crappies in streams takes place in middle to late fall, when the fish congregate around sunken brushpiles, weedbeds, fallen trees, and practically anything else which attracts and holds

Fishermen in the northern states can enjoy a twelve-month season when slack backwaters freeze thick enough to allow ice fishing. This angler jigged a rubber-legged ice fly for his crappie catch. Courtesy Illinois Conservation Department.

schools of minnows. Unlike spring fishing for crappies, fall angling usually takes place in the stream's deeper sections, although cover remains the major object.

The white crappie *(Pomoxis annularis)* is found over nearly all of the United States but is predominant in the South and Midwest. It has six spines in the anal fin. Black spots on the fish's silvery sides are arranged in seven to nine vertical bars; the black crappie's spots are randomly arranged, giving the fish a speckled appearance. The white crappie has a somewhat more elongated body shape than its black cousin. Wherever found, black and white crappie have picked up nicknames, including calico bass, papermouth, and slabs, the last name usually being reserved for crappies which exceed 2 pounds in weight.

The white crappie prefers murky, silted rivers and streams, but can tolerate either hard or soft river bottoms. The black crappie *(Pomoxis nigromaculatus)* is choosier, however, preferring clear, cool waters with hard rock or sand bottom.

Whether white or black, however, crappies are school fish, and finding one usually means finding a bucketful. In streams, look for crappies in the largest pools with only minimal movement of the current. Young crappies feed on plankton and insect life (both aquatic and terrestrial), and adults move on to raw meat, preferring minnows and the fry of other stream fish. Black crappies are strictly carnivorous and are suckers for minnows, crayfish, and large insects. Schools of crappies often spend the summer moving slowly up and down a particularly suitable pool, nabbing insects from the surface, corraling minnows, and doing more loafing than anything else.

Come fall, however, when the autumn leaves stain river waters, the crappies once again school tightly and head for deep-water brush to feed exclusively on minnows. Stream crappie fishing then is identical to lake crappie fishing. You need only locate a good sized brushpile or drowned treetop in fairly deep water, and you should find dozens of hungry crappies feeding heavily in preparation for winter.

In the Deep South and Florida, a favorite way to catch stream and river crappies is to troll very slowly along shorelines lined with weeds, using a live minnow on light line and a cane pole. This puts the bait through the maximum amount of cover and is a relaxing way to fish as well.

Large numbers of crappies are caught on artificial baits too, of course, and this is my favorite way to catch them. I like a very light fly rod, tapered line, and 9-foot leader tied to a 1/32-ounce Doll fly. If the crappies are near the surface, especially in midsummer, I switch to almost any pattern of white dry or wet fly, such as the Coachman or Miller. Spinning also takes a lot of fish, with small spoons and jointed fly-rod plugs favored.

Whatever method you use, however, remember the crappie has a very fragile mouth, easily torn if the hook is set too smartly or the fish is horsed. And if you fish live bait (minnows) near submerged brushpiles, it can save tackle and tempers if long-shank, soft-wire hooks are used. These hooks are easily straightened by a pull on the line if they become snagged way down under, and can then be reshaped and used again. If you fish live minnows effectively for crappie, you *will* become snagged occasionally. If not, you're fishing in the wrong place.

Use caution when approaching and anchoring near submerged brushpiles thought to hold fish. Crappies are wary creatures and will stop feeding if overly disturbed, and even leave the area completely if the fisherman isn't careful. If you're fishing from a canoe or cartop boat, shut off the motor well away from the cover and drift into position, making sure the boat doesn't nudge the brushpile. Oars should be muffled and onboard items like tackle boxes, coolers, and such should be carefully stored to avoid banging them against the gunwales. All the care and attention pay off when you've located a school of crappies gorging on minnows, however.

Old-time crappie anglers call brushpile angling "vertical fishing" because baited lines are lowered straight down through the brush to where the crappies are located. Often no more than 5 feet of line extends from the rod tip and only the tiniest of bobbers is used to detect the light hit of a crappie taking the minnow or Doll fly. Once you've hooked your fish, waste no time in hauling it straight up and into the boat, as this helps prevent the fish from fouling line around submerged cover and avoids alerting other fish in the school. It's not unusual to take two or more dozen crappies from a single large brushpile in fall, if care is used; one crappie expert I know caught a verified total of 346 slabs in three days of fishing the brush on a new state lake not far from my home. All were taken on live minnows and came from a total of only *four* brushpiles!

Bluegills are suckers for a rubber spider fished with a fly rod. Find an active school and you'll stop fishing before they stop hitting.

PUMPKINSEED

If ever God created a panfish especially for small children, it has to be the pumpkinseed *(Lepomis gibbosus)*. This brightly colored little stream fish, found over much of the country, seldom grows to lengths greater than 8 to 9 inches but is easy to catch on a variety of baits, is fine table fare, and is probably the most highly colored panfish in U.S. waters.

The pumpkinseed's head is bright red with bluish stripes radiating from nose to gills. The gill flap is blue-black and bears a dark spot edged in red. The dorsal area is olive-black and the belly is bright red. Anal and pectoral fins are pale yellow, and the dorsal fin is bright olive-yellow. The fish's mouth is rather small for its size, a fact which should cue the fisherman to select baits in the correct size range.

The pumpkinseed usually remains near shoreline cover in large, slow-moving streams and small rivers, preferring the security of standing vegetation, sunken tiles, fallen logs, and similar objects. I have often found the highest concentration of these fish in such easily fished spots as large root systems half-submerged in water, where large shoreline trees grow. Such spots are easily reached by youngsters fishing from shore and often hold several of these bright little fish.

Pumpkinseeds have a rather broad diet, apparently restricted only by the small mouth. Snails, insects, worms, grubs, and small minnows and fry will catch them, as will slowly retrieved fly-rod spoons, wet and dry flies, small Doll flies, and tiny ultralight spinners. A simple cane pole rigged with monofilament line of about 6-pound test, a No. 10 wire hook, and a canful of redworms or waxworms will outfit the angler for pumpkinseeds, be he six or sixty.

REDEAR SUNFISH

Call it redear, bream, shellcracker, or stumpknocker, you're still talking about a popular and beneficial little sunfish with an odd addition to its anatomy well adapted to a special diet.

Streams, like ponds and lakes, contain concentrations of crappie where submerged logs provide cover. A light canoe reaches such places with ease.

The redear, found widely over the eastern half of the United States, is a popular substitute for bluegills when new lakes and ponds are to be stocked because the redear is not the prolific breeder its bluegill cousin is, and therefore does not overpopulate the waters where it is found. Redears have been known to crossbreed with bluegills, in some cases producing surprisingly large, sterile hybrid offspring.

The redear's diet of mollusks (snails) accounts for its unique set of teeth located on the rear surface of its tongue. These teeth are used to grind the snails, shell and all. The fish also eats insects, crayfish, and some minnows, but it is the habit of eating snails which gives it the nickname of shellcracker.

In ideal waters (especially in the South) redears may weigh 2 pounds and measure 12 inches in length. The tip of the gill flap is reddish—bright red in male fish and orange in females. The pectoral fin is long and pointed, and the body is stocky.

In streams, redear sunfish are infrequently found around submerged cover, but the larger fish, those of most interest to fishermen, seem to prefer open water in large, slow pools away from persistent current. The fish are only loosely schooled for most of the year, concentrating noticeably only in May and June when spawning occurs.

Lepomis microlophus is caught on a wide variety of baits and artificial lures, including (but not restricted to) catalpa worms, wasp larvae, waxworms and redworms, plus small wet flies, panfish bugs, and rubber spiders in small sizes. They are game little fish that deserve to be caught on tackle light enough to make the best of their spunky fight.

GREEN SUNFISH

The green sunfish, also called blue-spot or green perch, is seldom sought out specifically, because of its uniformly small size. Even in the most ideal habitat, these little stream panfish seldom exceed 6 inches in length, and an 8-incher would be exceptional. Rather, the fish are taken by light-tackle anglers after bass, southern stream trout, and other, larger panfish species sharing the same stream.

Lepomis cyanellus is common all over the Eastern United States and has been introduced to such Western states as Colorado and New Mexico. Its coloration is a brassy olive-green with pale vertical bars and a creamy white belly. Its lips are rather large and rubbery, and the anal fin contains but three spines.

The greenie, as it is called hereabouts, favors rather small, rocky streams and can thrive in surprisingly little water. It prefers the area of slackening current just below sections of riffles and is therefore found alongside smallmouth bass. Found in small schools near good rock cover, green sunfish can often be taken one after the other on the smaller spinners of the kind that are used for bass. The species is tolerant of murky, silted water.

Greenies, as their habitat suggests, dine considerably on hellgrammites found in their rocky home, plus small crayfish, nymphs, adult insects, and small minnows and fry.

The crappie is often called Old Papermouth because of the thin membrane in its mouth parts, which requires a delicate touch.

The little fish will hit small, slow-moving flies, spinners, and fly-rod spoons, plus such naturals as live hellgrammites, redworms, and grubs. The plentiful greenies are considered pests by flyfishermen seeking smallmouth bass.

ROCK BASS

There is a definite warm spot in my fisherman's heart for the rock bass, sometimes called the poor man's smallmouth. Without a doubt the game little rockie has saved more days astream for me than holiday bonuses saved Christmases.

Early-morning hopes of finding leaping bass sometimes faded, then mutated into satisfaction when I happened across an eager school of these stripe-sided panfish among the rocks and rubble of bass streams from southern Canada to the Gulf Coast. It seems the rock bass are always there, always willing, whenever the smallmouth develop lockjaw for my lures.

In fact, this very thing happened barely three weeks ago as this is written. Two friends and I were wading a favored smallmouth stream, and try as we would, no big smallmouth ("big" on this river means 3 pounds) could be found. Finally, in a stretch of flat water sliding through a watery field of rocks, George Kellar happened to drop a cast across a particularly thick cluster of half-submerged rocks. Immediately a half-pound rockie nailed his BeetleSpin bait. Another cast, another fish, and so on. There, less than 50 yards from where we'd parked the car three hours before, was a rock-bass honeyhole less than 20 feet wide but positively loaded with panfish varying between 8 and 11 inches long. There was nothing particular to mark the spot in the amber water, yet the rock bass had congregated there in unbelievable numbers. When we finally departed, we'd caught 27 rockies and called it a day only because the sun was already behind the treeline and not because the fish had stopped taking our artificials.

The only unusual feature of that spot could not be seen in the dark water and was discovered purely by accident. George permitted one cast to sink a bit far and his bait caught on a rock. When he waded in to retrieve it, he was suddenly standing in waist-deep water, fully twice as deep as the water less than 15 feet away.

Rock bass, I now believe after some twenty-five years of stream fishing, locate amazingly small sections of streams meeting their needs and remain there nearly all of the time. Perhaps temporary forces such as floods or drought will move them out for short periods, but they soon return with normalized water conditions. In several Midwestern rivers I have fished, rock bass seem to form small schools in pocket water just off the main current, particularly when such spots are broken with plentiful rocks and perhaps rimmed by low-growing willows.

The rock bass, *Ambloplites rupestris,* has a Latin name well suited to its habitat. The species name literally means "on the rocks," and it is here you will find the rockies. Perhaps this has something to do with alkalinity of special importance to the fish or its natural foods; I quite honestly don't know. I do know that rock bass very often show up in my creel after a

Crappies and their favorite food: minnows.

day's smallmouth or spotted-bass angling, and even after a session of stream trout fishing in some of our Southern states.

The rock bass is probably second in greatest potential growth only to the black and white crappies. The state record in Ohio, which contains a great many rock-bedded streams, is presently just ½ ounce under 2 pounds and nearly 15 inches in length. Rock bass can grow to very good size for panfish, although the species has the deserved reputation of fighting well when hooked but giving up quickly thereafter.

Called goggle-eye, red perch, and redeye in various parts of the country, rock bass are found from southern Canada all the way to the Gulf of Mexico, and are more prevalent in the eastern half of the nation than in the west. The fish's body is rather stocky, with dark olive on the dorsal surface fading to a dull white on the sides, sometimes with pale-olive bars arranged in vertical formation on the sides from dorsal to lateral line. The eye is often a deep red. The mouth is large and extends beyond the eye. Rock bass have six spines in the anal fin and eleven or twelve spines in the dorsal fin.

As might be guessed from its preferred rocky habitat, the rockie eats small crayfish (hardshell or softshell), hellgrammites, insects and their larvae, and small minnows and fry. The fish will respond to a fairly fast retrieve, faster than is effective for most panfish, and therefore are often caught by smallmouth-bass anglers using wet or dry artificials.

Rock bass favor the wading or canoeing angler because their habitat is often found in midstream. Once found, however, an honest-to-gawd honeyhole can keep the rod bent and the kids happy until the moon comes up.

WARMOUTH

The first time I ever caught a warmouth I thought it was a one-of-a-kind freak of nature. The head looked altogether too large for the body and the mouth was ridiculously large. And I remember thinking the fish's facial appearance made it look particularly pugnacious. Neither assumption turned out to be accurate, of course, but, let's admit it, the warmouth *does* look a little odd.

The range of *Chaenobryttus coronarius* stretches from Minnesota through the Great Lakes, south to Texas and Florida, plus some waters on the West Coast. The fish has a large

This bluegill fell for a small brown nymph retrieved slowly just off bottom. Such a nondescript fly pattern will take many kinds of fish.

mouth, thick lips, a stocky body, three anal spines, and teeth on its tongue. A dull fish, the warmouth bears an olive-gray, mottled coloration with a reddish eye. Maximum length is about 11 inches with the average about 6–8 inches depending on habitat.

The warmouth, actually a type of sunfish (as are all panfish herein, plus the black basses, for that matter), prefers murky water with a good deal of natural vertical cover and a soft mud or clay bottom. It is particularly fond of dense weed patches and can be taken by bait and lure fishermen concentrating their efforts around large "fields" of duckweed, water willow, and other thick-growing aquatic plants.

For all of its melodramatic name and appearance, the warmouth really isn't much of a battler, even on light tackle. But it is a willing eater and can be tempted by crayfish and their tails, snails, gobs of worms, and wet flies and small spinners fished slowly. Look for these fish in larger streams and slow-moving rivers, especially in the deeper pools containing vegetation.

RED-BREASTED SUNFISH

It was one of those long, warm South Carolina evenings when the crickets were in good voice and it seemed to take forever for the black-silhouetted trees along the Edisto River to fade into a purple August sky. I'd planned to spend all of my Carolina visit fishing for the famous largemouth bass of the Santee-Cooper country, but a friend and local resident talked me into spending a couple of days on the Edisto River, about 25 miles south of Santee, South Carolina, not too far inland from St. Helen Sound.

"Ah know fishin' for sunfish doesn't sound *rilly* excitin' but these red-breast of ours are *rilly* somethin'," said my host. And who would have refused? My casting arm needed a rest, anyway.

We floated a 30-mile section of the Edisto those two days, never seeing another angler or even a parked car. What we *did* see was the hottest panfishing yours truly has ever had anywhere. And not little fellows, either; some of those red-breasts *(Lepomis auritus)* weighed nearly 2 pounds. I was *rilly* impressed.

At my host's urging, we tried both live and artificial baits. We caught fish on live crickets, fish on redworms, fish on ultralight spinners, and fish on fly-rod poppers, thoroughly enjoying these gamest of panfishes and forgetting all about those 10-pound bigmouth back in the lakes.

Before leaving the subject, I should add that South Carolina's Little Pee Dee River is also excellent for sunfish, and the species is found in many of the state's other blackwater rivers and streams. In fact, the country's best red-breast fishing is found in streams and rivers in the huge Atlantic drainage.

The red-breast, known as sunperch and bream in the South, is reminiscent of the pumpkinseed in coloration, but grows larger and is a much better battler. The species' distinguishing feature is its long gill flap, which is usually tipped with dark blue. The head below the eye is striped in light blue from the nose rearward to the edge of the gill surface, the back is dark olive with broad vertical bars, and the belly is red or orange-red breaking into red spots toward the tail.

It doesn't take fancy tackle to catch stream panfish, especially sunfish and bluegill. This father-and-daughter team caught enough to make both of them happy.

Red-breast males fan beds in gravel in spring when water temperatures reach the mid-60° mark, fan the nest during incubation, and care for the fry for a short time after hatching. Like the bluegill, the male red-breast is most possessive of his spawning area and will savagely attack any intruder, including a well-cast bait.

Unlike most other panfishes, the red-breast can be taken at night, and hits most any type of small artificial or live bait with gusto. Naturals which are effective include worms, catalpa worms, small minnows, and hellgrammites. Effective artificials are often whatever's in the box—small spoons, wet and dry flies, spinners, and even ultralight wobbling plugs.

Generally speaking, where identical panfish species appear in both ponds and streams, the larger fish are produced in ponds. This is true of such species as bluegill, crappie, and pumpkinseed. The rock bass, green sunfish, and warmouth are generally considered moving-water fishes and do far better astream than in stagnant-water lakes and ponds.

So why fish for panfish in streams at all? Why not catch them in larger sizes from ponds if you fish for them at all?

I suppose the answer to that is that where you fish is very much a matter of personal choice. I fish for stream panfish first because I like stream fishing, preferring it over slack-water angling, and second because, unlike some other stream fish, panfish of one kind or another will bite all year round, not just in spring and fall. I've become quite fond of ultralight fly and spinning gear, and this gossamer gear makes the most of a panfish's spunk as it burrows for bottom or turns its wide side to the rod tip and weaves a circular battle.

Certainly there is no better or more forgiving teacher of basic fishing techniques than the plentiful panfish, undoubtedly accounting for the great American stereotype of the barefoot boy walking down a dusty road with one hand carrying a tomato can of worms, the other a cane or willow pole. That lad is on his way to catch panfish. No doubt about it.

My two daughters, ages eight and four, are still discovering the joys of catching as many bluegills as we have bait for from a nearby limestone stream. The look on their faces when they bait a hook with a squirming redworm, the rapt attention paid to a wiggling bobber, and their delight when the float disappears and a raised rod tip pulls a thrashing bluegill from the water—on stuff such as this are lifelong memories built.

And of course there is no law that says the old man can't sneak an ultralight spin outfit along in the unlikely event the kids stop catching fish long enough for a cast or two or three to be made.

SMALLMOUTH BASS

There is no way of telling how many cases of mumps had to settle for delayed treatment, or how many babies had to deliver themselves, during the last quarter of the nineteenth century in Cincinnati, Ohio, but chances are the numbers are considerable. At least, this would be true among the regular patients of one Dr. James A. Henshall, a general practitioner of the period who, judging by his devotion to the smallmouth black bass, must have spent as much time on bass streams as modern doctors spend on golf courses.

Henshall's *Book of the Black Bass* is the first tome dedicated entirely to this great gamefish of stream and river and stands even today as a remarkable example of research and insight. Henshall loved the smallmouth, laboring over its "proper" Latin name with more care and fretting than did any newborn's mother left to fend for herself when the good doctor was off on an angling trip.

The name the book finally settled on sounds stiffly proper: *Micropterus dolomieu*. But, owing to a very limited closeup look at the fish to be named, the Latin monicker is all wrong.

The word *micropterus* means "small-fin," a description which does not fit the smallmouth's dorsal fin at all. As it happened, the specimen chosen for examination by its namer had suffered some sort of injury or birth defect, because a portion of its dorsal fin was missing. But the men of the time knew nothing of this and chose the inordinately small fin upon which to found a name. The Latin name's second half, *dolomieu,* merely refers to a French friend of the man who chose the fish's name.

Some question existed as to whether the fish ought not be named after its cousin, the largemouth bass *(Micropterus salmoides),* but enough anatomical differences were noted between the two so that two Latin names were rendered.

Even the modern descriptive name for this great bronze battler isn't entirely accurate. In fact, only a third of its proper name, "smallmouth black bass," is right. In the first place, at only one stage in its life, and then only for a very short time, is the smallmouth actually black. The fish is colored black only during the "swim-up" stage shortly after hatching, whereupon it turns its characteristic green-brown.

Nor is the fish a true bass, technically speaking. In fact, the smallmouth, like the largemouth, is a member of the sunfish family and not a bass at all. Some experts insist that the only *true* bass in all of North America is the white bass *(Lepibema chrysops),* but that's another argument.

There are as many colloquial names for the smallmouth as regions in which it exists. Green trout, trout-perch, bronzeback, brownie, smallie—all refer to the smallmouth, and usually with affection. But virtually wherever it exists, at least a few common characteristics set it apart from its largemouth cousin.

Generally speaking, the smallmouth is a more handsome fish. Its colors are varied, with the dorsal's olive brown fading into dark vertical bars from the gill flap to the base of the tail. Two or three olivaceous bars, originating at the eye, are situated fanlike to the rear of the gill. The eye is generally red, and the overall body shape is slimmer than the largemouth's.

The rearmost edge of the bronzeback's mouth never extends past a point midway through a vertical line drawn through the eye, while the largemouth's mouth extends to or beyond the rear edge of the eye. A closer examination of the

Missouri's Eleven Point River, a fine bass stream, is one of the original eight rivers in the national wild and scenic rivers system.

two fish will reveal another, more positive difference between the two. The smallmouth's dorsal fin is continuous and contains only a shallow notch between the front (spiny) half and the rear (soft) half. The base of the soft dorsal carries small scales, while the largemouth bass' rear dorsal carries no scales at all.

I would also say that if you caught first one type of bass and then the other, the fish which fought harder and longer would be the smallmouth, but with all the largemouth anglers out there, to do so would be risking attack with drawn fillet knives. We all have our little preferences.

The smallmouth is a spring spawner. When stream temperatures reach into the middle to upper 60s, it migrates upstream in search of a gravel bed suitable for spawning. This may mean the nearest bed, if the male bass finds it meets his needs, or it may mean the fish will move into a much smaller tributary creek which holds sufficient water only during spring flooding. I have found spawning bass in creeks and brooks barely 5 feet across, busily going about the ritual of reproduction.

Once a suitable gravel bed is located, the male smallmouth fans out a shallow depression, or redd, then leaves the site for short periods while he searches for an egg-laden female, which he drives to his nest by hazing her in the right direction and sometimes nipping her flanks to hurry her along. The female deposits some of her eggs and the male then drives her away and searches for a second female, and the process is repeated. Up to three separate female smallmouth may deposit eggs in one nest.

The male then fertilizes the eggs (averaging about 2,000), and the eggs hatch in from two to nine days, depending on water temperature. Unlike its largemouth cousin, the smallmouth does not stay around to look after the newly hatched fry, but departs shortly after fertilization occurs. The young smallmouth, after hatching, are left to fend for themselves. They are pitch-black, save for the gold-colored iris of their eyes.

Once the bass fry has swum up, it is on its own. It seems there are predators everywhere: mature smallmouth quite willing to devour young of the species, rock bass, channel catfish patrolling the shallows, even large crayfish alert for anything that passes within reach. Survival to maturity is denied most of the newly hatched smallmouth, yet enough reach sexual maturity to ensure future generations.

At first the young smallmouth must eat tiny crustaceans in its limestone-bedded home stream. The diet ther progresses to the larval and mature stages of insects, crayfish, and finally minnows and small panfish. How soon the young bass reaches catching size depends upon the fertility of its home stream and the average temperature of the water. Some smallmouth have been known to reach 9–10 inches in as little as two years, while bass found in less ideal water require up to seven years to reach the same length. The fish may require up to ten years to grow to the trophy class of 18 or more inches in length.

The smallmouth's ideal habitat is somewhere between that preferred by trout and largemouth bass. A good bass stream must have at least some current, preferably broken here and there by riffles, which add oxygen to the water while providing breeding habitat for both the smallmouth and its prey. The stream should contain pools considerably deeper than the riffles, and plenty of in-stream cover, such as fallen logs, rocks, willow beds, gravel and sand bars, and even some manmade structures. Some of the hottest bass fishing I've found has been around and under old bridge pilings, sunken concrete tile sections, and even tractor tires left where past floods had taken them.

Although a limestone bedding is not a hard-and-fast requirement for smallmouth streams, I mention it because rivers and streams which flow over at least some limestone deposits seem more biologically active than other streams, containing a wider variety of animal life which, in turn, better supports a stable bass population.

Smallmouth are thought to prefer their water a bit cooler than their largemouth cousins, and it has been my experience that in streams where both species exist, the smallmouth will dominate in terms of both individual growth rates and sheer population.

The smallmouth also seems able to thrive in smaller streams than the largemouth. Give the bronzeback a few feet of water depth, a limestone ledge or rock to hide under, and an occasional crayfish or hellgrammite, and it's there for life.

Knowing what the smallmouth eats should be high on the list of priorities for anyone making a career of seeking this fine gamefish, and the list is long. Among the items on the smallmouth's menu are hellgrammites (the larval stage of the dobsonfly), crayfish, minnows, small panfish, sculpins, moths, beetles, grasshoppers, caterpillars, frogs, and the fry of their own species. The smallmouth is a predator, and nature won't let the fish forget it. Keep this in mind when choosing a live or artificial bait and when fishing it.

There are definite times of day during which stream bass are most active. Early morning and later evening usually find these predators prowling the shallow, rocky shores and heads

The vertical bars and small mouths on these Tennessee River smallmouth easily determine them from largemouth bass.

and tails of riffles for any unwary creature small enough to make a meal. During midday, the larger smallmouth usually continue their solitary habits by retreating to favored lairs offering protective cover, shade, and a position from which the fish can flash if food moves near. In fact, the most productive method of locating heavy smallmouth, particularly at midday, involves reading the stream to pinpoint likely holding spots, then fishing them carefully.

A good friend of mine is a master at the art of finding unusually large smallmouth in his home stream. Harold Barefoot, a canoe concessionaire near my home town of Englewood, Ohio, fishes the Stillwater River with great success year after year, attributing his success to knowing smallmouth habits and combining this with a thorough working knowledge of the stream.

Harold believes in taking his bait to the fish, and this means casting his spinners and floating-diving plugs so close to good bass cover that the bait often scrapes bark or rock on the way back to the canoe. This is often the difference between hanging several good fish on his stringer, or having to settle for middling-sized smallmouth taken from less ideal cover.

I can't count on both hands the number of times Harold has accurately predicted that he will catch a good bass from such-and-such a drainage tile, sunken log, submerged rock, or gravel shoal. "There's a good fish ri-ight a-bout . . . there!" he'll say, leaning back into a fish suddenly all fight and fury and spending more time over the water than in it. If I didn't like the guy so much, his success would get on my nerves.

Years on the water with Harold and other good smallmouth anglers have taught me the very real value of first reading the water, then planning your approach and cast to match the circumstance. When fishing the head of a pool, for example, take a few minutes to survey the water you're about to fish before even your shadow falls on the water.

Most riffles, because of their turbulence, produce a bit of foam, which is carried into the pool below before dissipating. This foam line usually marks the path the current takes and, in turn, the path taken by food carried by the current. In early morning and late evening, bass often patrol the waters in line with and to the side of the foam line, waiting for the current to deliver dinner. At midday, look for half-submerged logs and rocks near the foam line in deep water; such spots are prime holding areas for lone smallmouth, usually the largest in the river.

The deepest sections of the pool usually hold few large smallmouth, unless unusually good cover, such as an entire fallen tree or jumble of large rocks, is there. Only on rare occasions have I found many bass in such spots, and then only during the hottest summer months when the bass' usual holding spots get just too warm for comfort.

Bass rivers and streams (the difference often lies in local terminology rather than stream size) quite often include flat sections of swift, slick water just above the point where riffles break up the current. Bass often cruise slick water above riffles. This seems to be a favored location for both minnows and bass; thinking back, most of the minnows I have seen fleeing bass, sometimes actually skipping over the water in a panic to escape the predator below, have been in that accelerating current in the crossover water between the tails of pools and the beginning of riffles.

Never pass up the chance to take advantage of an actively feeding bass. Often the fish is more vulnerable to a bait even faintly resembling the creature being pursued. Fleeing minnows, of course, are easily imitated by any number of artificial baits—white or gray streamer flies, Muddler Minnows, Rapalas, A.C. Shiners, BeetleSpins, and small spinnerbaits. And of course, the angler outfitted with a pail of live minnows need only hasten to bait a light hook with the minnow and drop it gently several feet upstream from the feeding smallmouth. Chances are the bait won't drift far before you'll have a fresh-hooked smallmouth out there arguing with you about his civil rights.

Almost any type of light- to medium-weight freshwater fishing tackle will catch smallmouth bass. The choice of which rig to use depends partly on the water to be fished, and partly on the fisherman's own preference. But if you forget all else, remember that the smallmouth bass is a predatory creature. Like a housecat, the smallie is excited by lifelike movement, so fish that bait, real or artificial, in a lifelike manner.

Most magazine articles I've seen are written by people who so favor flyfishing for bass that they seem to forget that most light-tackle anglers today prefer the more easily mastered open-bail spinning outfit. Let's face it: You can toss extremely light baits with properly balanced spinning rigs, and the outfit enables you to switch from live to artificial baits and back again with only a change of knots. No wonder so many people use spinning tackle—it's darned near perfect.

Many stream fishermen seeking bass do very well with a light- to medium-action fiberglass spinning rod of 6½ feet total length, an open-bail reel such as the Cardinal 3 or 4 or the Garcia 308 or 300, and monofilament line testing from 4 to 8 pounds. This very versatile outfit is seen everywhere from California's Russian River to the Connecticut River watershed of Vermont. Although the smallmouth is more likely to stick around and slug it out in close quarters than to make long runs, it's a good idea to set your reel's adjustable drag so that it engages when a force of slightly less than half of the line test is applied. For example: line test 6 pounds, drag set for about 2½ pounds of pull; line test 8 pounds, drag set for about 3½ pounds of pull, and so on. I prefer to use the blue or clear-blue monofilaments on today's market, rather than the brightly colored yellow and orange types. Maybe I'm the exception, but I'll be darned if I can catch bass consistently on the new colored lines.

Spinning lures which catch bass are as numerous as stars in the heavens on a June night, but I have some favorites which produce virtually wherever I fish for bronzebacks. Among the true spinners I like the No. 1 Mepps, 1/16th-ounce and 1/8th-ounce Rooster Tails with bronze blades, the ¼-ounce Abu Reflex, and the old reliable Presca Perch with surgical-tubing body. As a rule of thumb, I find that bronze- or copper-bladed spinners work best in very clear water, while the flashy silver- and nickel-plated blades do the best job in dingy stream water. Dull-finish blades also seem to attract more bass in shallow water than do the bright models. Here's a tip: You can rejuvenate scratched and tarnished spinner blades by dabbing a bit of common toothpaste on a soft cloth and buffing the blade until it shines. The toothpaste contains mild abrasives which really do the job on dull blades. As far as I know, no one knows the effect of the paste's flavor on a hungry smallmouth bass.

Lord knows there is a plethora of bass plugs available to the modern angler, but you can quickly reduce their number by a third by size alone. The stream smallmouth lives in a much smaller world than its largemouth cousin in its lakes and reser-

Never ignore in-stream cover where a lunker may be hiding. This calls for accurate casting, but a fish worthy of your den wall is worth it. Courtesy Mercury Marine.

voirs, and won't tolerate the explosion of a large hunk of hook-festooned plastic or balsa slamming the ceiling of his home. Smallmouth plugs are smaller than most, with the weight of ½ ounce being the absolute upper limit. And while the river's biggest bronzeback may occasionally welcome a 6-inch jointed plug fitted with flashing lights and a siren, the best stream plugs are those which alight on the water with a minimum of splash and closely resemble some morsel regularly eaten by the bass, be it a frog, grasshopper, minnow, or whatever.

Some of the plugs I've found very effective for stream bass include the smaller minnow-imitating balsa baits, ⅓-ounce crankbaits in brown, green, and cream colors, and the old standby lead-head jigs in black. When the bass are deep and finicky I have found ⅛-ounce jigs dressed with a bit of dark-colored cloth cut in tiny strips to be very effective, particularly when fished carefully around sunken cover, which often hides lethargic fish in hot weather.

Another hot-weather trick calls for combining flyfishing with ultralight spinning gear. Equip a whippy little spinning rod, say up to 5½ feet long, with an open-bail reel and 4-pound or 2-pound monofilament. Using the surgeon's dropper loop knot, add a dropper line of about 15 inches above the end of your line and tie on a pair of unweighted marabou streamers, one to each line end. Add one or two very small split shot and drop the rig wherever you suspect a bass in holding. You'd be surprised how this ultralight approach moves big bass into striking when the heavier gear goes glimmering. And battling a big, strong smallmouth on this cobweb gear comes very close to the ultimate in sport. You don't actually *defeat* the fish, you *coax* it into submission.

A fishing friend of mine, Karl Maslowski of Cincinnati, has been fishing small streams for smallmouth for over thirty years and has quite a few notable fish for his efforts. Karl uses the 6-inch sinking plastic worm a good deal of the time, but disdains pre-rigged worms in favor of preparing them himself. Using a large needle and a foot or so of 6-pound monofilament line, Karl rigs the worm with two No. 6 hooks by threading the line from the front to a point just behind the collar, or dark ring, around the worm. One hook is securely tied in there, and the threading continues to the worm's rear end, where the second hook is tied off. The original end of the monofilament is then pulled, which imbeds all save the hooks' bends and points inside the plastic worm body. The rig is finished with a small snap swivel tied in the line just ahead of the front of the worm. Karl prefers natural worm coloration for his creation, and fishes it weightless on spinning tackle, casting it here and there and making a slow snap retrieve through likely cover. A stream Karl fishes, barely 30 feet across in some places, has produced bass up to 4 pounds with this rig.

Flyfishing for stream smallmouth is pursued as avidly as the trout purist seeks rainbows. In fact, so well adapted is the fly rod for this gentle art that many fishermen consider it the only truly proper way to seek this species. Little wonder, the facts being that stream bass live in rather shallow water and will come to a fly-rod bait, wet or dry, with the same willingness as a trout, and often with more power.

As this is written, I can look across my typewriter to a corner where a favorite fly rod awaits only a willing hand. It is rigged with a stout monofilament leader of moderate taper, and one of the hottest local smallmouth flies is knotted at the ready. Called the Old Ugly, the pattern was found in an old fishing annual and turned over to my fly tier for reproduction. The flies he tied vary from light beige to all-black and, for the lack of a better description, look like Muddler Minnow heads with a marabou tail. Like a Muddler, the Ugly can be fished just under the surface or, if weighted or fished on a sinking-tip line, down a few inches. It seems to resemble a sculpin or crayfish and has been most productive when fished in fairly shallow water just below riffles or near in-stream cover. If I was limited to one fly for smallmouth, the Ugly would be it.

Two other flies which have served well for subsurface bassing are the aforementioned Muddler and the large dragonfly and hellgrammite nymphs. I like the fur-bodied Muddler tied to sizes 8 and 10 on a 4X hook, and the big, dark nymphs from sizes 6 to 8 2X. All these flies take a great many bass, particularly in the slow-moving bass streams typical of the Midwest and South.

The rod for smallmouth flyfishing needn't be anything special. Its length is determined as much by the water to be fished as anything else. Brushy-shored streams may require the use of shorter rods because of the lack of backcasting space, and for this I use a little 6½-foot glass wand. But any rod between 7½ and 8½ feet long, and with a bit of backbone to turn over the seldom-bulky bass flies, will serve well.

The fly line, as far as I'm concerned, need only be matched to the rod and of good enough quality to withstand a season of being draped across flat rocks and occasionally snagged on cottonwood branches. If kept dressed, virtually any line will do. I use weight-forward or double-taper lines, the former for hair bugs, spiders, and other top-water baits, the latter for nymphs, dainty dry flies, and streamers.

Leaders need only be of moderate length unless the stream you fish is unusually clear. I get away with 6 feet of tapered leader (5X) for wet fishing, and perhaps a point 2 feet longer for the dries. Both are available commercially or you can tie up your own, trying different formulas, although this is a chore I have found unnecessary for river bass.

When flyfishing for bass, fish *toward* something. Unless chasing minnows or spooked out of its lair, a big bass seldom strays very far from its solitary haunts, preferring to lie in wait like a cougar after a deer. Often a hungry river bass will take up a vigil in pocket water, those serene little pools off the stream's main current and perhaps sheltered by a half-circle of willows or large rocks. As a crappie is drawn to submerged treetops because they contain minnows, so is the smallmouth drawn to pocket water containing sculpin, green sunfish, small rock bass, and crayfish. Keep your presentation light, casting near the edges of the pool, and use a snappy, darting retrieve, as if your bait were a small fish fleeing the bass. Pocket-water fishing is perfect for ultralight spinning gear or the ever-ready fly rod.

Like most people, I suppose, I caught my first-ever smallmouth not on artificial bait, but on the real McCoy. My father and I were camping for a summer weekend on a secluded little limestone stream which emptied into the Ohio River, and although we welcomed any bass we happened to catch, our main target was channel catfish, which often inhabit the same water. We'd been using live hellgrammites for bait, having caught them by hand the day before and kept them alive overnight in a large, shallow pail with a little water and a few rocks added.

Our method was simple: Hook the hellgrammite through the tough collar just behind the head on a "bass hook" (in those days any hook made of stout steel and having a short shank was called a bass hook), add a bobber 36 inches above the bait, and cast this rig at the foot of riffles and let the current carry it downstream. If no taker was encountered, the rig was picked up and cast again.

On one drift the bobber moved sideways in the current a foot or so, then was pulled out of sight. I struck, up came a 15-inch smallmouth instead of a catfish, and although the tackle I was using was too heavy to give the bass an even chance, the fish's two jumps enroute to shore were enough to start a love affair with this fine gamefish which has yet to cool.

A braggin'-sized string of smallmouth bass from Pickwick Dam on the Tennessee River. All of these fish hit deep-drifted baits of live minnows. Courtesy TVA.

Live bait will sometimes outfish artificials, particularly when the bass aren't actively feeding and need a bit more time to look over an offering before deciding to eat it. This is in the natural way of fishing live bait, with the retrieve slow enough so the bait itself wiggles, kicks, or swims in a seductive manner.

Crayfish, also called crawfish, craws, and so on, probably make up at least 50 percent of a stream bass's diet, simply because they are plentiful in most bass rivers, because they are relatively easy to chase down and eat, and because of the creature's habit of discarding the old exoskeleton (outer shell) three or four times a summer as body growth demands it.

When the crayfish feels the need for a new shell, it moves into shallow water, away from the current, and the old shell is slowly removed. Once free of the old protection, the naked crayfish can move only very slowly for several hours until the new shell is formed. Many dedicated bass fishermen are joined by bait dealers in believing that smallmouth bass prefer softshell crayfish to those with fully developed shells, but it is my belief that softshells are simply easier for the bass to catch, and that, once caught, the bass cares little whether the creature has a hard shell covering or not. The *size* of the crayfish does matter, however, and this should be considered when you capture your own bait or buy it at a bait store. Whether the bass you fish for average 12 inches or 2 feet long, crayfish from 1 to 3 inches total length will catch them. Even an unusually large bass will, it seems to me, more readily take a bite-sized bait than a real mouthful, particularly at times other than the peak feeding period.

The crayfish, whether hard or soft, is hooked from below in the base of the tail so that the entire hook point and barb extend above the upper tail surface. This hooking method will catch most bass which take the bait (a bass usually takes the entire crayfish in its mouth when striking), and has the added advantage of reducing snags because the hook point rides *up*. The only change I make in the crayfish, and then only in the larger ones, is clipping off the pincers. This probably makes little difference to the bass, but it can save pinched fingers for the chap on the other end of the rod.

Hellgrammites can often be the best-producing live bait a smallmouth angler can use, provided these dobsonfly larvae are native to the particular stream to be fished. This is easy to check. Just wade out in the nearest riffle, choose an area of moderate current where the water is flowing a few inches deep over plentiful bottom rocks, and slowly lift the *upstream* edge of any flat rock. Hellgrammites vary from 1 to 4 inches long, have flat, black bodies, many sets of legs, and a large pair of pincers on the front part of the head. When disturbed, the creatures roll up into a ball and loose their grip on the rock, permitting the current to carry them downstream to the safety of another rock. Hellgrammites can be hand-captured (watch those pincers) or collected in a seine (see chapter on natural bait).

Hellgrammites can be especially effective when fished at midday on very light line and little or no added weight. I like

Ohio fisherman Harold Barefoot brings a 3-pound bass aboard in his beloved Stillwater River. Barefoot knows the best spots and catches good bass regularly.

to use a light wire hook, impaling the creature just behind the head; this permits it to live quite a long time on the hook. These creatures are very tough and will sometimes catch two or more bass before needing replacement with a fresh bait.

Drift-fishing a hellgrammite is similar to drifting a spawn bait for steelhead, but on a smaller scale. The unweighted hellgrammite is cast well up into the riffles and allowed to drift at river speed into the riffle's tailwaters and into the pool below, imitating an unfettered creature which has become dislodged from its home under a rock and which is fair game for any bass along the feeding lane.

In rivers with a fair current, the hellgrammite fished in this manner won't have the opportunity to fasten itself to a rock and stop the drift before you retrieve and cast again. In streams with very slow current, however, you may want to clip off the hellgrammite's rearmost two pair of legs and its pincers to keep it from stopping the drift by grabbing a passing rock or log.

When a bass takes the hellgrammite, chances are it will grip only an inch or so of the bait while making a short run. Open the bail of your reel quickly and pay out line. When the run stops or slows, wait a few seconds, then snap the bail closed and strike hard. The bass should have the entire hellgrammite and hook in its mouth and a solid hook-up will be assured.

Nightcrawlers are another excellent bait for river bass, and require a somewhat softer rod, particularly in the tip section. Large worms intended for river fishing are usually hooked only once, through the dark-colored collar a third of the way between head and tail, and it takes gentle casting to avoid losing the bait before it hits the water. Nightcrawlers are drift-fished in much the same manner as hellgrammites, except that smallmouth bass usually take the entire bait in their mouths immediately, so it isn't necessary to let them run before striking.

Worms can be a very hot offering during and just after a rainfall which raises the stream level a few inches and/or colors the water a bit. Summer rains very often wash streamside worms into the water, and bass are on the lookout for them. The same applies to stream trout, panfish, steelhead, catfish, and, to a lesser extent, even salmon.

Minnows take a great many bass, and can be fished either deadline (without a float) or a couple of feet below a light bobber. I have found, at least in the Midwest, that minnows are most productive when fished in the stream's quieter backwaters and eddies, rather than in the strongest current. Maybe this is because minnows living in the stream are not strong enough to fight the current and therefore inhabit the easy-living waters themselves.

I prefer a very light, short-shank wire hook and little or no added lead weight, because the more freedom given the minnow to swim in a natural, untethered manner, the greater its attraction to the bass. I like to use a very small round plastic float a few feet above the minnow, as it gives me greater control when drifting the bait close to in-stream cover suspected of harboring bass. There are excellent commercial floats available for this purpose, and two good ones come to mind immediately. The Dayton float, made of hollow plastic and colored red and white, has a small button which, when depressed, exposes a small brass hook on the float's opposite side, where the line is attached. Adjusting for various depths is quick and easy, and the float will not slip out of position once attached. The second type is homemade and consists of almost any small bottle cork (fishermen always have plenty of bottles around) with a hole punched lengthwise. The line is threaded through the hole before the hook is attached, and a wooden matchstick is pushed halfway through the hole. The pinch of the cork against the matchstick keeps the float at the desired level, yet the depth is easily adjusted.

Whatever type of float you choose, keep it small and light. Large floats are not easily towed around and can quickly deaden the minnow's fish-catching action.

From its original range from Ontario south to Georgia and northeast to Maine, the smallmouth remains the same great gamefish which lured Jim Henshall out of his doctor's office nearly a century ago. Today, through extensive stocking programs, the smallmouth is found in nearly every state, a few Canadian provinces, and even in the Far West streams of three Hawaiian islands.

The following list of smallmouth streams and rivers by no means covers all of North America's watercourses containing bass populations, but is meant as a guide to the blue-ribbon streams which provide consistently high-quality bassing.

ALABAMA: Entire length of the Tennessee River in Alabama, with the best smallmouth fishing in the upper area of Pickwick Lake in the tailwaters of Wilson Dam.

ARKANSAS: Buffalo River in north-central Arkansas, and the upper reaches of the Ouachita River.

CALIFORNIA: Top waters include the Napa River and Alameda Creek, Putah Creek and the Russian River, tributaries of the Sacramento and San Joaquin River, including the Feather, American, Stanislaus, and Merced Rivers.

CONNECTICUT: Tributaries of Waumqumbaug Lake, Pocotopaus Lake, and Lake Zoar on the Housatonic River from Brookfield through Oxford.

DELAWARE: Brandywine Creek in northern Delaware is the state's top bass water.

GEORGIA: Tennessee River drainage, plus tributary streams of Lakes Blue Ridge and Chatuge.

HAWAII: Wailua River system on Kauai, two tributary streams of the Wahiawa Public Fishing Area on Oahu, and a few small streams on the island of Hawaii.

IDAHO: Snake River from Twin Falls to its mouth, Clearwater River from Kooskia to its mouth, and the Salmon River from Riggins to its mouth.

ILLINOIS: Many streams in the state's northern half provide good fishing, with the Fox River system probably tops.

INDIANA: Tippecanoe and Pigeon Rivers are good, as is the Whitewater River in the southeastern section above and below the new Brookville Dam and reservoir.

IOWA: North to South along the Mississippi River on the west, Little Sioux River and the chain of lakes headed by Silver Lake; on the eastern side along the Missouri River are the Turkey and Volga Rivers, Maquoketa River and Buffalo Creek, and the Iowa River north of Eldora.

KENTUCKY: The Bluegrass State is blessed with a vast network of small to medium-size bass streams; among the best are the Cumberland River and Rolling Rock Creek.

MARYLAND: Potomac River, from Little Falls near Washington, D.C., upstream to Cumberland in Allegany County. Western Maryland, with its mountain watercourses, is generally considered the state's best area for stream smallmouth in quantity.

MICHIGAN: The St. Joseph River contains catchable smallmouth, as do a number of smaller streams emptying into Lakes Michigan and Huron.

MINNESOTA: The Root, St. Croix and Blue Earth Rivers, plus the Wolf River, are among this particular state's top smallmouth streams.

MISSISSIPPI: The Tennessee River system in the state's extreme northeastern corner is excellent in the vicinity of Pickwick Lake.

MISSOURI: The Ozark region, in Missouri's south, offers fine smallmouth fishing in its Gasconade, Meramec, Current,

Eleven Point, and Elk Rivers and their tributaries, plus the Osage River below Bagnell Dam.

NEVADA: Carson and Humboldt Rivers, plus the South Fork of the Owyhee River; in the 1960s bass were stocked in the Bruneau River.

NEW JERSEY: Tops is the Delaware River in Mercer County.

NEW MEXICO: 20-mile section of the Rio Grande River above the junction of the Rio Grande and the Chama Rivers north of Espanola.

NEW YORK: Delaware River and its West Branch, the tributaries of Lake George, and the big St. Lawrence River.

NORTH CAROLINA: The state's western third is tops, with the Green River and the New River in Ashe and Allegany County probably the best of the lot.

OHIO: In the south, Whiteoak and Eagle Creeks, from the Ohio River to their headwaters; in the west, the Little and Great Miami Rivers and their tributaries (East Fork Creek near Batavia is among the best). A federal fish hatchery at Senecaville produces 270,000 smallmouth annually, most of which go into Ohio streams.

OKLAHOMA: The Mountain Fork, Little, and Glover Rivers are good, as are the tributaries of the Grand and Illinois Rivers in the state's northeastern region.

OREGON: Three rivers containing smallmouth are the Snake, Middle Fork of the Malheur, and the Columbia.

PENNSYLVANIA: Three rivers are tops, although bass are found in smaller streams practically statewide: Allegheny, Susquehanna, and Delaware.

TENNESSEE: Nolichucky and Buffalo Rivers in their entirety.

VERMONT: The Connecticut River system in the western region.

VIRGINIA: Try the streams in Botetourt, Carroll, Grayson, and Highland Counties.

WEST VIRGINIA: Among the fifty-two streams containing smallmouth bass, probably tops are the South Branch, Greenbriar, Elk, and Cacapon Rivers, and the Fish and Wheeling Creeks.

CANADA

ONTARIO: The network of streams and rivers along the lower Great Lakes watershed, Rainy River, and the St. Lawrence system.

BRITISH COLUMBIA: Mainland, Kettle River; Vancouver Island, Cowichan River.

QUEBEC: North and west of Ottawa—Hull in Abitibi, Gatineau, Pontiac, Timiskaming, Labelle, and Papineau.

NEW BRUNSWICK: Mostly in the southwestern part of the province, including the St. Croix River and the Chiputneticook chain.

MANITOBA: Upper Winnipeg River, Whiteshell River, and Bird River.

STREAM TROUT

The stream world of the trout is not that far removed from that of the smallmouth bass. Both depend on their habitat for food, cover, a place to spawn, and some variation in depth and water temperatures during extreme weather.

Even the habits of the three basic kinds of stream trout—rainbow, brook, and brown—are similar to habits displayed by the bass. Each is a predator and should be approached as such by the hopeful angler, whether he's armed with a 2-ounce fly rod or a fresh-cut willow pole. Make that bait, live or artificial, appear like the real thing in front of a feeding trout, and it's yours.

But what, I can hear you thinking, about all the lore surrounding trout fishing I've heard about? What about upstream casting and 10X leader points and keeping your shadow off the water? Was all that just *bunk?*

Well, yes, partly. Trout fishermen, like no other group of civilized men, like to straitjacket themselves with more so-called protocols and traditions than any English court, and very often such rigid rules are simply not needed at all.

Take, for example, one morning I spent on the lovely little Frying Pan River, a few miles above Basalt, Colorado. I would have felt more at home with my trusty little ultralight spinning rig and a handful of proven spinners, but I knew my companion was an avid flies-only addict and in deference to him had chosen a fly rod with which to flog the foam.

We fished for three hours without so much as *seeing* a trout. Nymphs with and without weight in the channels and chutes of white water, dark and bright streamers in the slicks, fragile little dries on the quiet water, and all on cobweb leaders cast with the sun in our faces.

No trout. Not even a swirl or a bump or as much as the disheartening sight of another flyfisherman taking his first of the day. I trudged back toward the car heavy of heart and light of creel.

"Good morning!" said a voice from among some streamside aspen trunks. "They're really hungry today, aren't they?"

I finally located a middle-aged woman seated comfortably on a red sandstone rock. She was using a tiny spinning outfit rigged with gossamer line and a tiny wire hook not as long as my thumbnail. On it she was impaling single salmon eggs, which were cast diagonally upstream and allowed to sink as they drifted slowly past. And piled at her right ankle were seven trout, not a one under 12 inches long. Her catch included at least one each of the river's four kinds of trout—rainbows, brookies, browns, and cutthroats, the last called "natives" there in the Centennial State.

I suppose my gawking moved the woman to elaborate. "Just catching my breakfast," she said, retrieving another salmon egg from a small bottle and nonchalantly rebaiting her hook. "My husband's upstream a ways. He fishes for big trout with his flies, but I can't wait on him for breakfast, so I'm catching my own."

While continuing my trek to the car, I naturally began salving my ego with the standard little ego-salvers: The fish she's catching were probably stocked in the river just last week, and she's using salmon eggs when the rest of us have to use flies, and if this were a flies-only stream she couldn't do that. I have all sorts of little rationalizations which nicely avoid the fact that I've been skunked. We all do.

Hard to reach and tough to fish, this Western trout river will probably continue to provide blue-ribbon fishing for decades to come.

But the simple fact remained: The woman using bait was *catching* trout while I was *chasing* them. I could admire the admittedly lovely Frying Pan Valley, its redrock and aspen, its soaring eagles and puffy white clouds, but the fact wouldn't go away: I came all the way out here from Ohio to catch trout and I'm not doing it. I'm beating myself to bruises wading over sharp rocks and through swift currents, and that woman is just sittin' over there and catchin' her breakfast, casual as you please.

And *that's* when I started to question all this crap put out by lifelong dedicated trout fishermen who will, if you let them, proceed to dictate how you shall fish, with what you shall fish, and where you shall fish.

I told myself that back in the Midwest, people go fishing to catch fish, not to look at the birdies or stare at a rock. So what's the big difference when they go afield after trout? Sure, trout are special, but only because they require water not above a certain temperature and therefore can't survive in the Florida Keys. The same equation applies elsewhere. Have you ever heard of a tarpon being landed, say, in Minnesota? Not recently you haven't, but that doesn't mean you can't fish for tarpon any way you like, just so long as it's legal and the fish like it.

The catch in all this opinionated pap, of course, is the fact that, on many days and in many situations, drifted salmon eggs or garden worms or cheese balls just will not catch trout, particularly when these primitive predators are feeding heavily on, say, such insects as mayfly or caddis larvae, minnows, grasshoppers, salmon flies, or any of a hundred or so other creatures which make stream trout grow fat and sassy.

For the trout, for all its gullibility to worms and such, can be a mighty selective critter. This is often helped along when the water in which it lives is pounded seven days a week by a fiberglass army of anglers bent on matching wits with the fish, the stream, the overhanging trees which snatch sloppy backcasts, and their own inept manner of wading into a pool as if they were landing at Normandy.

Brown trout, said to be the wariest and toughest to catch of stream trout, *have* been taken by barefoot kids drowning worms under a bridge, but more often the lunker old brownie will spook when the shadow of your leader touches his nose and he's down for the time it'll take you to fish out the pool and stomp off through the cornfield. The lovely brook trout, that dumb denizen of what remains of North America's cold, clean streams of the Northeast and the mountainous West, will often turn up its handsome nose to anything larger than a No. 18 dry tied perfectly on just the right fly hook. Even the rainbow, our most commonly stocked trout, can be pretty finicky at times. Lord knows I've emptied three fly books and still managed only to put down the very rainbow I'd been trying to tempt for over an hour.

I know of no study on the matter, but I am willing to guess that at least 75 percent of the trout finning in America's streams this very minute started their life in a hatchery under the watchful eye of some fishery biologist, rather than having risen from a bed of pea gravel. The ages at which these fish were stocked in the thousands of streams varies, of course; some states stock when the fish are still quite small, giving them time to become stream-smart before having to encounter the angler's offering of hooks, feathers, and worms. Other states, such as Ohio, where I live, prefer to retain hatchery trout until they reach catching size before placing them in the wild.

Whichever is the case in your state, however, it remains to the credit of the trout itself that it can undergo pellet feeding, inoculation, tank trucking, and stocking, yet retain enough of its heritage to become, very often, incredibly particular about what it eats, how it eats, and how much disturbance it will tolerate before scurrying for the bottom.

So perhaps, after all, the trout addicts have a point. When *any* fish is finicky it is just good sense to alter your fishing methods to match the needs of the moment. If that big brown only comes out from its rock to feed at night, you either fish for it at night or you go home skunked. Or perhaps that dainty and wild brook trout you've spotted in some beaver pond in backwoods Maine must be fully convinced that the bug on the surface really *is* a mosquito larva, and that means a 12-foot leader and a super-cautious presentation.

Outdoor writer Jim Robey tries his hand at drifting a weighted nymph under midstream cover on the Roaring Fork River. Pockets of slack water in a big, fast river often hold good fish.

Maybe the point I'm trying to make is that I believe in fishing for trout in the manner dictated by the fish, not by some stuffed-shirt legion who claim direct lineage back to Izaak Walton. If someone wants to use freshly dug earthworms while I use, say, a No. 18 Ginger Quill, so be it. Even the purists must admit that, chances are, even *they* caught their first dozen or so trout on a gob of worms and a cane pole. Where they go wrong, I believe, is dragging the rest of the angling world along when they graduate themselves to the use of flies only. It may just be that the rest of the world doesn't want to go.

A young friend of mine, who ties the most beautiful and accurate trout-catching creations ever lashed with a whip finish, is only seventeen years of age and already a snob. We were fishing a nearby trout brook one winter day when we met a lad of perhaps a dozen years probing his worm bait under brushpiles and overhanging banks for the river's willing rainbows. "Just look at that!" scoffed the older youngster.

"He's caught three trout on worms. People shouldn't be allowed to fish for trout like that!"

Never mind that we'd been throwing feathers since dawn with no luck, the worm fisherman was wrong because he dared to buck the pressure to conform. Seventeen years old and a full-blown snob. What'll he be like by the time he's reached fifty?

Tolerance, tolerance.

Let's take each of the three major trout species one by one, and maybe we can discover how to fish for each with at least a modicum of success.

The rainbow trout *(Salmo gairdneri),* as it appears in most North American streams, is a handsome creature. Its back is colored a bluish green from snout to tail, fading to silver on the sides and finally to creamy white on the belly. Most domestic strains are heavily spotted with black from the dorsal surface to the lateral line. The fish gets its name from the red lateral band which starts just below the eye and ends at the base of the tail. Dorsal and adipose fins, plus the tail, are olivaceous in color, while the pectoral, ventral, and anal fins are varying shades of pink, with a few black spots interspersed near the base.

The rainbow is perhaps the most commonly stocked domestic trout because of its high tolerance for elevated water temperature and the relative ease with which it can be reproduced and raised in hatchery situations. The steelhead trout is actually just a much larger version of the rainbow, but steelhead strains have a stronger urge to migrate. Domestic and steelhead rainbow strains are sometimes found in the same stream, but the smaller rainbows are permanent residents while the steelhead that you find there have just stopped in to spawn.

Compared to other stream trout, rainbows are usually found in those parts of the stream containing the fastest water movement. This is not to say that you're likely to catch 'bows halfway up a whitewater cascade, but they will likely be not too far from the foot of such chaos, tucked contentedly away in some protected pocket water from which they can flash if the current serves up dinner.

German brown trout are considered the perfect quarry for fly enthusiasts, but that doesn't mean they won't hit a lively plug now and then. The author's brownie weighed 6 pounds and was caught in Wisconsin.

The rainbow is a great jumper and fights well in all but the smallest sizes, given properly light tackle. And it does the usual trouty things—it rises to floating insects when they are abundant, sometimes leaping completely out of the water in its haste to capture a mayfly or a moth, or your floating fly. The rainbow also has a special fondness for a variety of underwater items, especially the very common caddis larvae and pupae and the cases they construct from whatever materials are available on the stream bottom.

The rainbow also eats crayfish, minnows and dace, sculpin, and a variety of "blow-in" terrestrial insects dropped on the stream by summer breezes, including grasshoppers, caterpillars, ants, moths, beetles, and crickets. When it rains and nature makes them available, earthworms are added to the rainbow's diet. The rainbow is not a creature of parochial tastes, although his preferences are sometimes determined by what is available at the moment.

The same can be said of the German brown trout, an import from Europe first placed in a major American stream (Michigan's Père Marquette River) in 1883. Since then the brown, generally considered to be the most difficult of trout to catch on a fly, has been successfully introduced in some forty-two states and nine Canadian provinces. It was the brown trout which rescued flyfishermen in America's Northeast when their favored brook trout declined as the result of deteriorating water quality. Today the brown has become *the* quarry for many Eastern trouters, although a goodly number still hold out for the wild brookies of upper New England.

The brown trout *(Salmo trutta)* has made a fool of me on occasion (which puts me in a very large company). One fine June afternoon on Arkansas' White River, a stream known for its plentiful rainbows and trophy-sized browns, I was float-fishing a stretch near Mountain Home. The river was its usual slick, smooth self and the rainbows were willing if somewhat small. The guide, a down-home retired farmer who knew the river well, suggested we try one of his favorite and (he claimed) secret spots for a big brown trout no one had yet boated. The 'bows were small, I had yet to hang a heavy fish, and so we moved.

The guide's comfortable 20-foot johnboat was beached on a gravel bar and I was directed to fish the currents around a tangle of fallen trees in midriver. "If he's out an' feedin' you won't have any trouble seeing him 'cause he's purty big," was the guide's last remark as I waded away. The trout was active, all right. His broad, rubbery-looking tail slapped the surface regularly as he came up to slurp at the debris flowing by. Through several inches of clear river water his bronze side looked a foot wide. It was not the kind of situation in which my heart does a regular seventy-two per minute, and my first cast showed it, slapping the water and propelling a large,

The rainbow trout has been stocked in American waters for well over 100 years and still provides the bulk of the nation's trout fishing. It is easily handled in hatcheries, adapts well to stream life, and fights well with many jumps.

dark dry much too hard. The cast put the fish down for a couple of minutes, time enough to recover lost line and start false-casting for the next rise.

I couldn't see what the fish was taking, but it was small. I broke off the big dry and tried a No. 16 Adams. This brought a swirl from the fish, but he only nosed it as it went by. Another drift and the fish rose and slurped heavily, and my fly disappeared. I struck, the rod bowed in his direction, and the fly came loose.

To this day I don't know whether that fish actually inhaled the fly or the point merely scratched his snout long enough to bow my rod. I do know that it was the biggest brown I will ever drift a fly over. What rankles me is, brown trout do that sort of thing so regularly, as if their mission were to humble trout fishermen.

The brown is especially well suited to a life astream. Its tiny scales exude a special mucus which coats its skin and reduces friction while controlling the absorption of water. Dorsal color is a brownish bronze, fading below the lateral line to a yellow-white on the belly. Red and black widely spaced spots, often ringed in light blue, prevail from the dorsal down the sides past the lateral, and the tail and fins are colored a gold-yellow. Another identifying feature is the brown's double row of vomerine teeth, located in the roof of its mouth on the mouthpart called the vomer. Hatcheries handling both brown trout and Atlantic salmon sometimes use this method to differentiate between the two because other body features among the fry of both species are similar. The Atlantic's vomer contains only one row of teeth.

Unlike the rainbow, the brown trout prefers the larger, slower pools, particularly those containing a considerable amount of in-stream cover in which the fish hides until later evening or full dark, when most of the heavy feeding is done. A few hundred yards of Michigan's Platte River fit this description and contain very nice fish. The stretch is surrounded by nearly impenetrable cedar swamp just upstream from Platte Lake, and must be fished from a small boat capable of negotiating the river's twists and turns. But the river here offers several big hatches of caddis flies every summer, making the trouble worthwhile. The pools are big and deep; the cover is heavy, and so are the fish.

Perhaps for the very reason that browns can be so tough on flyfishermen, they have become for many the quintessence of the art. In the East, where anglers have had decades to develop them, certain patterns have become standard among brown-trout devotees. The list would have to include such dries as the White Wulff, Hendrickson, Quill Gordon, Light Cahill, Adams, and, to a lesser extent, Joe's Hopper and a few of the thickly hackled skater patterns.

In the West, as with many things in Big Sky country, patterns preferred for brown trout are larger than elsewhere, owing to the larger size of natural nymphs and emergent insects found on big Western rivers and even the tiniest mountain brooks.

A good bit of the brown-trout flyfishing done in the West is of the wet type, using what to Easterners appear to be positively huge Wooly Worms, Ribbed Hare's Ears, and other

Hatchery-raised trout show amazingly tame behavior before reaching the stream. These young rainbow froth the water when food is presented.

hefty patterns. Streamers like the White Marabou also take a goodly number of browns each year, particularly when the rivers are roiled and full of snowmelt during late spring.

A friend of mine, invited to fish a private stretch of the Roaring Fork River one June, later reported having seen a big brown gathering insects in a manner I had not heard of before. Along its banks the river wore a heavy skirt of mountain grasses, which overhung the water and nearly touched the surface. A swirl caught the angler's attention when a large brown sailed slowly up and down the pool just under the surface. He swears he saw the brown swat tufts of overhanging grass with its tail, then turn about for another pass, during which the insects dislodged by its tail were gathered up like so many fallen acorns in an oak woods. He said the innovative brown fell for a large Joe's Hopper dropped just ahead of its nose.

Local chapters of Trout Unlimited and other flyfishing clubs, particularly in the Northeast and mountainous West, have succeeded in having prime sections of trout rivers designated Flies Only. Coloradoans have gone one step farther and added a regulation requiring that all fish measuring 12 or more inches taken from some flies-only sections must be returned to the river unharmed. This is an attempt to maintain high-quality flyfishing while permitting the fish to reach maximum size. It also avoids the necessity of asking the state to restock that particular stream section as often as the put-and-take water.

A Midwestern flyfishers' club has thus far been unable to get a flies-only section on local trout water, but has done the next best thing to improve the quality of angling. They have assigned each club member a beat on the stream to be stocked. Each man is equipped with a sort of portable livewell for trout, which is filled with several dozen adult fish from the state tank truck. Wearing waders and being careful to keep the trout in his care underwater, the member wades downstream on his beat, using a small dipnet to place one trout under this cutbank, two under that brushpile, another in a deep slick. This spreads the available trout over a wider stretch of river and prevents schooling under the numerous bridges where state fishery workers used to dump an entire load of trout. The method also makes the maximum natural foods available to each stocked fish.

One species of fish, the brookie, has not been stocked in quite the same numbers as its rainbow and brown cousins. The brook, not a trout at all but a char, requires the coolest year-round water temperatures of the Big Three. Water readings cannot exceed 75° F. at any time, and cooler water from springholes, never exceeding 62–65° F., must be available to the fish. This country's history of defoliation, permitting sunlight to penetrate where it never penetrated before, has permanently raised stream temperatures in the East and Northeast, pretty well wiping out the brookie in favor of the more tolerant brown trout.

But where they prevail, brookies have a way of garnering angler affections. And no wonder, if only for looks alone. The wild brook trout, taken from a high mountain stream in the Rockies or some back-country creek in New England, is a lovely thing. The fish's dorsal is a dark olive with red spots ringed in blue, and the entire dorsal and lateral surface is mottled with wormlike olive-yellow lines called vermiculations. The belly is cream-white, and fins are bright pink with white edging along the frontal surfaces. The brookie's nickname of squaretail is derived from the unique rear edge of the tail, which has little or no indentation.

Today's best brook-trout fishing can be found in the rivers and lakes of Labrador, Argentina, certain rivers in Maine, and God's River in east-central Manitoba, where brooks may *average* four pounds. In the Western United States, many rivers, small streams, and lakes have become overpopulated with brookies, because of the species' ability to reproduce.

Sometimes the fish can become so numerous, and therefore undersized, that they can become a nuisance. I recall just such a circumstance on Goose Creek, a tributary of the Rio Grande River not far from the New Mexico–Colorado border. Elk, the object of our hunt, were still in their summer range among the peaks, giving me time to explore the little ribbon of water at our camp's door. The creek contained the usual four types of trout—browns, rainbows, natives, and brooks—plus a few small salmon said to migrate from a private lake nearby, but try as I could I caught five brooks for one of any other species. The squaretails were everywhere, stacked like hungry

Bill Slivinski fishes several tiny streams, usually with bait. Here he admires a 17-inch rainbow which hit a live worm in midwinter.

cordwood in every pool, lurking in every riffle, ready to pounce on anything resembling food. Another hunter and I used Golden Hare's Ear nymphs and a tiny gold spinner to keep the entire ten-man camp in fresh trout for the week.

Brook trout can be seen taking insects from the surface, and truly tiny dries seem to be the best bet here. Among the brook's chief menu items are ants, beetles, grasshoppers, and caterpillars. It also eats a great many aquatic insects, such as the nymphs of caddis flies, stoneflies, and mayflies, as well as a number of small baitfish found in their waters. Wet flies for brookies are invariably of the strawberries-and-cream type—bright, rather bulky attractor patterns such as the Silver Doctor, Royal Coachman, and Montreal. Streamers favored include the Light and Dark Tigers, Mickey Finn, and Nine-Three. Nymph patterns are usually dark in shade and should closely imitate emergent insects.

Quite a few brook trout are taken every year on flashy hardware—spoons, wobblers, spinners. I think this type of bait is so effective because the brook's diet contains a rather large amount of small fish. Where legal, ultralight spinning lures which imitate baitfish can be deadly, especially where the brook trout occurs in large numbers, which is often the case in the West.

What trout eat, regardless of their species, is determined by what is available and catchable. This in turn is often determined by the type of stream the fish call home. If that water flows over soil and rock deposits which are of the right pH, aquatic organisms will be present in a wide variety, giving the trout a selection of available foods in good supply. If, however, the stream flows over such rock as granite and certain volcanic deposits, the stream bedding provides little in the way of added nutrients and the fish's food supply will be much reduced.

Hard-and-fast rules are always dangerous. No sooner are they drawn than someone comes along with an exception. But I will venture a rule here, or at least a definite distinction between trout waters, and if someone provides an exception, well, may it only serve to prove the rule.

Western trout streams are, by and large, rather sterile waters flowing over terrain which adds little in the way of life staples for trout. Called freestone rivers, they often originate high in the mountains and get their source from melting ice and snowfields, and from true springs seeping from between rocks and boulders. There is comparatively little food for trout in such an environment, and it follows that trout found there have a slow rate of growth and are rather few in number, unless supplemented by frequent stocking. Freestone rivers are susceptible to spring floods and sudden storms, and real gullywashers can flush available insect life temporarily out of the reach of the trout.

I was lucky enough one summer to arrive on the Roaring Fork River at Aspen, Colorado, less than a week after a late-spring snowfall had melted, raising the stream level a few inches and literally gouging the insects away. Having no insects to imitate made choosing a fly pattern tough, but it developed that a simple White Marabou streamer tied on a No. 10 hook caught all the trout I wanted, including one strangely unwary 2-pound brown which hit the dangling bait as it waved from an unguarded rod tip. I should add that I found all fish within 3 feet of shore that day, apparently unable or unwilling to fight the newly strengthened current of the river.

The foods available to trout in freestone rivers include the caddis and its nymph, small newts, stoneflies, mayflies, minnows, and small frogs. Among the more important in waters where they occur are unusually large stoneflies, often called salmon flies. *Pteronarcys californica* sometimes has a wingspan of nearly 4 inches and hatches in the spring on such waters as the Madison, Deschutes, and Yellowstone. The flies are quite large, and so are the trout which devour them so readily. Caddis Bucktails and the standby Wooly Worm in large sizes take their share of heavy trout when the salmon flies hatch.

Salmon-fly nymphs show a peculiar communal behavior when hatching, usually choosing a single large rock in a stream's particular section on which to crawl out of the water and shuck their old case. The new adult flies then fan their wings into position and fly off in twos and threes into the trees nearby. Trout, particularly the stream's largest, soon learn to hang around such rocks, picking off nymphs not yet free of the water and gobbling any unlucky enough to fall back into the stream after emerging.

In the East, rivers and streams are seldom of the freestone type. They are uniformly more fertile than Western streams, less susceptible to rain flooding and winter freezeup, and in consequence offer a much wider and more plentiful supply of natural trout foods.

And it's all because of tiny crustaceans called Foraminifera which lived countless millions of centuries ago, died, and deposited their carcasses in incredible numbers where they would undergo eons of pressure and become—limestone. Waters trapped among underground limestone deposits are more stable than freestoners, far more fertile, and have a narrower temperature range to a point well downstream from their source.

Actually, few rivers are *true* limestoners. The majority merely flow over surface limestone deposits, but even this factor adds immeasurably to the stream's ability to support trout. A limestone river usually has more varied aquatic plants than freestoners, including growths of watercress, elodea, and duckweed, which provide fish cover, add oxygen to the water, and stabilize the stream during high water.

Natural trout foods are plentiful in limestone rivers, and a partial list would have to include crayfish, caddis flies, stoneflies, mayflies, dobsonflies (and their nymphs), mosquito larvae, grasshoppers, moths, dace, sculpins, and fairy shrimp. Such a wide variety of available protein grows larger trout sooner and can support a greater abundance of fish in the same cubic measurement of stream.

Because insects make up such a large part of the stream trout's diet, I think it time well spent to look at the three insects of major importance to the trout, and therefore to the angler.

Insects which are born in the stream are available to the trout during two major periods in their life cycle: when they are in the nymphal and larval stages, and therefore completely aquatic; and during the brief period during and immediately following hatching and mating.

The three insect species of major importance—caddis flies, stoneflies, and mayflies—begin life on the stream bottom and its debris. They hatch from eggs deposited on the water and

A member of the Miami Valley Fly Fishers hand-stocks German brown trout in an attempt to establish a permanent brown-trout fishery. Members took off a day's work for the project, and provided their own equipment.

are in the form of very small worms having six legs and measuring no more than 1 inch total length. At about the same time every year, usually between late April and early fall, the nymph (worm) stage transforms into a pupa and begins to appear "buggy," with protruding eyes, discernible antennae, and jointed legs. Shortly thereafter, the pupa emerges from the water by various methods and sheds its shuck or pupal case. What emerges is the dun or as yet unmated adult, which soon flies away from the stream for a short time, usually making for streamside trees and bushes.

After a period which can range from as brief as an hour to as long as several days, the duns return to the stream to mate, often gathering in fluttering clouds just off the water, when they are known as spinners. The adult flies mate, and the females, after a very brief incubation period, deposit their eggs on the stream surface and die.

This, in a very brief and simplified form, is the life cycle of the mayfly, caddis fly, and stonefly. Each is of importance in the trout diet and certainly worth becoming familiar with if you plan to flyfish for trout at all.

The caddis is probably the most prevalent of the three stream insects. It appears in various forms numbering in the hundreds over a great deal of the United States and parts of southern Canada. The caddis worm is light-colored green or tan with a dark head and measures from 1/4 to 3/4 inch long. It clings to bottom stones and debris and makes up a large part of the trout's diet where present.

A unique habit of caddis worms is their construction of "houses" from nearly any building material they can find in the stream. These houses, which the worm hauls along until it changes into a pupa, look like little log cabins or stone chimneys and account for the bits of twigs and pebbles found in the fish's dietary tracts. The fish find caddis worms so delectable, they eat the worms houses and all.

Just how good trout find these little green worms was shown to me on Ohio's Mad River last summer. Three rainbows a companion had caught looked either full of eggs or bloated with food. When cleaned, the trout were found to be stuffed to the gullets with half-inch caddis worms. They'd eaten so many their bellies were distended, yet each fell for a fake caddis nymph fished deep and slow. Trout have shown themselves to be such suckers for caddis nymphs that I carry a dozen or so imitations in my fly book at all times. They are tied on No. 12 short-shank hooks with bodies of dubbed muskrat or mink fur, and can be real killers.

Ten days to two weeks before the caddis are to hatch, the worms seal themselves inside their little homemade cases and turn into pupae, which then depart the cases and move to the stream surface. Here the pupal case is shed and the adult

A quintet of rainbows from Colorado's famed Frying Pan River. This stream is both heavily fished and heavily stocked. It contains rainbows, browns, brooks and cutthroat trout.

caddis emerges. Newly hatched adult caddis flies display a unique hop-skip-and-jump behavior before takeoff, a movement which must be tantilizing to trout, because the fish eagerly rise to the hatched flies, often leaping completely out of the water as if afraid their quarry will escape. This is an excellent time to drop a caddis imitation near the most recent rise, although a wet fly resembling the rising pupa can also be effective, because there are usually those lazy trout which prefer to stay below to feast on the emerging pupae.

The adult caddis fly has no tail and holds its wings in the shape of an inverted V. Colors of the adult vary from light gray through tan. The hatches of these widely dispersed creatures sometimes last half a day.

Stonefly nymphs are found in fast, rocky riffles; they would drown if placed in still water because they breathe by means of tiny gills through which the current pumps dissolved oxygen. Trout look for the stonefly nymphs in the tails of riffles and the heads of pools just below these riffles.

The creatures emerge in early morning to midmorning by crawling out on half-submerged rocks. They seem to band together. A few rocks will bear dozens of stonefly shucks, while other rocks nearby are bare, making an angler's choice of fishing location an easy one. The adults have six legs, four rather long wings, and two tails, and stoneflies can easily be identified in flight because of the nearly vertical attitude of the fly's body.

Mayflies, the insect storied in song and fishermen's lies, are not as plentiful as the caddis, but there are probably more fly imitations of them than of any other ten aquatic insects. The Hendrickson, Quill Gordon, ad infinitum—all are designed to make trout think they are mayflies. And not only the trout like the mayfly; there are flyfishermen who will fish with nothing else and who seem to mistrust the motives of those who take trout by other means.

Mayfly hatches can come off from May through early September, depending upon the region where they exist. As a rule, the gray-blue flies come off first in the spring, followed by flies shaded yellow and then tan.

Whether you fish for stream trout with flies, hardware, or bait, however, the important thing is to fish where the trout are, not where they aren't. Trout in heavily fished waters are invariably more shy than those in wilderness streams, tending to remain near or under cover until food presents itself. This should give you a headstart when locating trout.

Fish the natural cover. Almost any half-submerged log, root system, undercut bank, or boulder has the potential of harboring trout if enough moving water is nearby. Fish which are away from cover and actively rising or showing their flashy silver color are easily seen and cast to; it's the fish which hide and wait you must seek.

If the cover lies along the side of the stream, chances are the trout will hold on the cover's side facing the current or in locations where the current passes alongside logs, rocks, or whatever. It is an easy matter, then, to position yourself across and slightly downstream from the cover, casting diagonally upstream from the target so the fly or bait drifts right under the noses of the hidden trout. Add one or two split shot above the bait as needed to keep it well submerged. Spinners fished in this situation should also pass by the cover and will bring better results if cast upstream and retrieved downstream, rather than the reverse direction. Trout seem to know that baitfish such as minnows and dace seldom move against the current for any distance.

When flyfishing the slow water on the far side of a fast current, it's a good idea to plan your move so your fly will remain in the holding water as long as possible. This is especially important to the dry-fly angler who must impart a natural dead drift to his offering if it's to be effective.

There *is* a way. On the final shooting cast, wiggle your rod tip back and forth as line is shot. This will put some slack in your line and keep your fly on target longer. You can also add 18 to 24 inches of 2-pound-test tippet material to your leader point; this will collapse on the water and give your overall line-leader a bit more length while you mend line upstream to prolong the natural drift of the dryfly.

Steadily rising trout can be timed, provided enough natural insects are on the surface. If you see a fish take a natural from the surface, get your offering where the rise occurred as quickly as possible. If the fish missed the natural, it will often take your fly without pausing to examine it.

In streams containing hellgrammites (dobsonfly larvae), trout eat them with zest. They can easily be matched with

Wisconsin fish biologist Lee Kernen shows his two-pound brook trout. Plentiful in a few areas, the brookie has been declared threatened in much of the Southeast.

slender streamers made of black marabou wing or any one of several patterns designed to imitate this vicious-looking stream dweller. As with most nymphs, hellgrammite patterns should be dead-drifted with the current, because live hellgrammites roll up into balls when dislodged from beneath rocks and permit the current to carry them to safety.

In states where it's legal, don't pass up the chance to fish for trout in winter. Small, dark nymphs fished very deep and slow catch trout in the cold months, and single salmon eggs and even garden worms do even better. Remember, trout are cold-water fish and are more active in winter than even the smallmouth bass. Fish the deepest water as slowly as the current permits with the lightest possible line. Winter streams are often low and super-clear.

In checking over my fishing notes for the past twelve months, I find that nearly half of the total trout catch came between October and late February, and the best single fish taken during that five-month period, a 23-inch, 5-pound rainbow, was caught on January 2 from a tributary stream narrow enough to be jumped with a running start. It fell for a No. 0 Mepps spinner with a chrome blade.

Winter fishing means getting out in the cold, often wading through fresh snow and putting up with freezing rain or sleet. But the dedicated trout fisherman soon forgets how cold he is when that tap on the line tells him he has a visitor. For a coldblooded creature, trout sure do warm me up.

SALMON

The wading fisherman found firm footing under his bootsoles, shook out several yards of fly line, and began false-casting. With each forward thrust of the powerful rod a few more feet of line stretched momentarily over the dark-green current where the river spilled between large boulders before flattening into a pool of slick water.

Finally the fly rod's forward movement carried it a few degrees above horizontal and the fisherman shot his line cross-current and slightly upstream. The long leader and the bright red-and-yellow feathers at its tip settled on the water, paused a moment, and sank as the full-sinking tip argued with the current over which would control the line. Each force had its say, and the line swept inevitably downstream, pulling its leader and bright salmon streamer sideways through the current, past a jumble of fallen boulders and into the pool's holding water.

The fisherman squinted a bit, eyeing his line closely as it entered the suspected hotspot, swept its length, and tailed out below. But instead of picking up the line immediately the angler let the fly hang in the current a few moments, then

Newfoundland's Serpentine River, a famed Atlantic-salmon stream, is so clear it permits fishermen to spot fish before casting. The Serpentine is near Corner Brook and is reachable via a private road. Courtesy Canadian Government Travel Bureau.

brought it back upstream in a series of small twitches. In his mind's eye he pictured the big streamer's marabou wings undulating with each twitch, but the retrieve was completed with no sign of a fish. Once again the false-casting was begun, line was shot, and another drift made past the boulders. The angler quietly sighed a bit and watched the line more closely this time.

The fish are there, he told himself. The fish are there, so keep casting.

The strike was not spectacular. The moving fly line merely stopped dead in the water momentarily. Fish or snag? The angler questioned only as long as it took him to raise the rod sharply and tighten the line. Suddenly the entire pool wasn't large enough for the freshly hooked salmon. An initial thrashing indignancy at the prick of the steel hook was followed by an upside-down leap clear of the water, another jump, and then a bulldogging run with the startled fisherman digging his heels in the riverbed sand while grabbing frantically for his reel drag adjustment.

Downstream 50 yards now, the big salmon used the belly of the bulky fly line against itself and made two more leaps. As he descended from the second leap the broad, silvery side pinned the leader between fish and current and with a small movement of its great head the salmon broke off. The lax line brought a fearful frown to the angler's face, and he quickly stripped in yards of line in hopes the fish was only running back upstream and was still hooked. Moments later, however, realization brought another sigh, a bit deeper this time, and the fisherman backed slowly toward shore and a smoke to settle his nerves and temper his disappointment. The now-empty leader tailed slowly back and forth in the current as if waving farewell to so worthy a quarry.

Salmon are the graduate course in an education which starts with sunfish, continues through bass and trout, offers an M.A. (Master of Angling) in steelhead and brown trout, and, for the dedicated supplicant, tops out with these great sea-run monsters come to call annually in the streams of both our coasts and the Great Lakes.

How big does a fish have to be before being dubbed "monster"? Relative size, like beauty, is in the mind of the beholder. I have no qualms whatsoever about claiming to have caught monsters when that catch included salmon of 20 pounds and above. In fact, I've done it several times, and those I've bragged to later didn't seem to mind when I said something eminently modest like "I tell ya, Bob, they were monsters!" Salmon do that to human vocabulary. They are, by and large, the biggest stream fish in North America, with the heft and raw power expected in fish which measure up to 60 inches long with a girth of half that. Salmon are bigger than life, heavier than the heaviest, strongest fish you ever thought you'd catch on that so-called heavy-duty fly rod or spinning wand. Freshly hooked salmon have produced more swearing than did the Second World War, and if the Good Lord ever tallies all my swearing and demands an accounting, well, I'll just smile weakly and mumble something about what 35-pound salmon do to my religious upbringing.

There was, I am told, an avid fisherman who died and stood outside the Pearly Gates while St. Peter looked over his admittance papers. The good saint found nothing that would keep the applicant from Paradise—in fact, he found the accounting blemish-free, and exclaimed of this to the mortal standing before him.

"Well, the record is not entirely complete, sir," said the painfully honest fisherman. "I once fished a great salmon river in Canada and hooked a fish which my guide said would easily surpass the current world record. As I battled the fish closer and closer to our boat, the guide searched in vain for the landing net. He rummaged from one end of the boat to the other while I became more and more certain I would lose that great fish.

"Finally, sir, I became very angry at his delay and I lost my head. 'You dolt!' I screamed at him in a towering rage. 'Where's that goddam net?' "

And St. Peter, leaning forward and obviously enthralled at the tale, replied, "Well, where *was* the goddam net?"

As I understand it, the chap made it into Heaven.

PACIFIC SALMON

Of the six species of salmon inhabiting the vast Pacific Ocean, only one is of no interest to fishermen—the cherry salmon, which spawns around the Japanese islands and does not provide sportfishing. The remaining five species are game enough and plentiful enough for even the most discerning angler. Largest of the Pacific salmon is the king (chinook), aptly named, undoubtedly, by someone who was impressed by overall size and brute strength. The king, like all salmon, has twelve or more rays in the anal fin and the king's mouth parts are always coal black and anglers are therefore frequently unsure when the fish they have caught sports dark-gray or slate-colored gums. The king often has a black spot on

Dour facial expression aside, Dick Martin of Shelby, Ohio, is mighty pleased with this hefty Michigan coho salmon. Coho are found in many Michigan streams each fall following the chinook runs.

the outer edge of the adipose fin, that fleshy little projection on the salmon's back between dorsal and tail fin. The king also has the widest anal fin of all salmon. Great Lakes fishermen, often confronted first by a king and then by a coho, distinguish between the two by lifting the fish by gripping its body just ahead of the tail. If the tail fin's upper and lower edges remain firm when the fish is lifted, the fish is a king. If the tail collapses, however, the fish is a coho (silver) salmon. And if the fish cannot be lifted without the help of a companion, the fish is most certainly a king—coho don't get that large.

The kings, like all salmon, are hatched far upstream from the sea in beds of pea gravel chosen instinctively by their parents. The gravel, with open spaces between each pebble, permits the water and its dissolved oxygen to pass over the fertilized eggs without washing them away. In late fall the eggs are deposited among the gravel, and in late winter they hatch. Still instinctively wary of predators, however, the new fry remain in their gravelly safekeep until the egg sac extending downward from their bellies has been consumed for food and they are forced to seek sustenance on their own. Only then do the fry reach what fisheries biologists call the "swim-up stage," lift out of the gravel, and begin the life of a free-swimming fish with three basic lifelong needs: food, cover, and comfort. This is all the salmon needs.

When a winter of feeding on plankton and microscopic insects has passed, the fry-turned-fingerlings ride the season's first spring flood downstream to the sea. In the Midwest, the Great Lakes have replaced salt water as the salmon's home during maturation. Once in blue water, however, king salmon sometimes travel well over 2,000 miles in search of the rich feeding grounds which in a few short years (three to five is the average) will transform them from 6-inch smolts to kings weighing up to 45 pounds in the Great Lakes and well over 100 pounds in Alaskan waters. Chris Batin, a correspondent of mine living in Anchorage, caught a king of 76 pounds from an Alaskan river on rod and reel, and a king reported to weigh 126 pounds came from another Alaskan river.

How do salmon find their parent streams up to four years after leaving it? Recent research has determined that smell has a great deal to do with the species' uncanny ability to home in on just one river or stream. Scientists claim that each river has its own peculiar chemical makeup. Only when the returning salmon locates that odor or taste which was long ago locked away in his makeup will it leave the blue water and turn inland to spawn and die. All Pacific salmon die after spawning, by the way; only the Atlantic salmon returns to the sea and back again to spawn more than once.

Once in home water, salmon soon lose their sea-bright coloration. The blue-black dorsal surface and silvery sides soon turn olive drab, and the salmon's black spots on dorsal and lateral surfaces and cheeks become more pronounced. In fact, I have caught salmon long astream and far from the sea which, when caught, looked somewhat like huge brown trout.

As spawning nears, more changes take place in the wearying fish. The male salmon develops the hooked jaw, or kype, and the hen fish's belly droops with its burden of thousands of ripe eggs. Once on the home gravel beds, cock and hen salmon join side by side over the redd, or nest. As the eggs are dropped to settle into the cracks and fissures between pieces of gravel, the cock fish releases his milt, which clouds the water for yards downstream if the fish is large. Soon thereafter, their purpose fulfilled, deterioration quickly follows, and the adult salmon lose vitality and die, their countless carcasses food for squabbling gulls, opportunistic bald eagles, and ravens. Those dead fish washed into deep water contribute their bodies to the nutrition of the river. So great can this glut of natural fertilizer become on small rivers, a biologist tells me, that one such stream, Michigan's Platte, has become a garden of lush aquatic plant growth in places because of nutrients released by decaying salmon.

To see miles of river shore lined with the rotting carcasses of salmon, the air full of flies and stench, is to have some concept of the strange ways in which this earth goes about replenishing itself. Old, useless creatures must die to make room for the vital and the young, but to see fish weighing up to 50

A 15-pound coho fell for this silver-bodied salmon streamer. Note the heavy-duty fly tackle needed for the job.

pounds lying dead seems to me a mockery of our meager conservation efforts.

The important thing is: Only two of the thousands of eggs a hen salmon produces need reach maturity to assure continuation of the species. The odds are long, but the eggs are many.

The five species of Pacific salmon include the king, coho, chum (dog), pink (humpback), and sockeye (red) salmon. And of these, only the king, coho, and pink salmon are considered of major sportfishing importance; the chum and sockeye are sought mostly by commercial netters.

Besides averaging well below the weight at maturity of the king, coho (silver) salmon are distinguished by the complete lack of spots, and, except for those on the back, the rear surface of all fin tips are edged in black. The base of the tail is wide and the iris of the eye is large. The coho has from nineteen to twenty-six gill rakers. A trophy coho weighs 12 pounds or more, with the average between 6 and 15 pounds in both the Great Lakes and Alaska.

The pink (humpback) salmon has very small scales and large, dark oval spots on back and tail. As with the king, the

The author and a nice salmon still bright from the sea. In many parts of the country salmon are the largest gamefish available.

base of the pink's tail is easily grasped and held by the human hand. Cock fish develop a very pronounced shoulder hump during spawning, and the upper and lower jaws develop pronounced kypes. A trophy pink weighs from 7 to 9 pounds.

Fishing for Pacific salmon, particularly the kings and cohos, is a matter of some discussion (and cussin') among anglers disagreeing on methods. Some fishermen swear by the use of spawn baits wrapped in mesh sacs (discussed in the Steelhead chapter), while others prefer to use only the eggs still attached by threads of membrane as they come from the fish. Plug casters also have their favorites, including such wobbling baits as the Flatfish, Tadpolly, and Hot Shot and such spinners as the Nos. 4 and 5 Mepps and other Colorado-bladed models. Flyfishermen clutch to their purist bosoms such a plethora of patterns and sizes and whole families of salmon flies that it would require fifty of these pages just to list each in agate type. But *all* effective salmon baits, whether natural or artificial, have one thing in common. They are taken by fish no longer eating to live, which brings up the still-unanswered, and consequently hotly debated, question, what makes a salmon strike?

It isn't hunger, for once the fish enters its spawning stream, feeding is forgotten as reproduction approaches. Some say it is irritation, which, they add, explains why an artificial bait must so often be cast again and again past a holding salmon before it deigns to strike it. Still others say the salmon is merely reacting to a lifelong instinct to consume available food, even though it is fat from gorging on smaller creatures in the sea. What makes salmon strike? I don't know.

A fisheries-biologist friend of mine suggests salmon strike artificial lures because of the bait's intrinsic bright colors and action in the water, plus something he calls "species pressure." When a half-dozen or more salmon are holding in close proximity in the same pool, their own group presence in so confined a space causes competition—competition for the best spot to rest and the best migration path upriver, and competition to possess that winking spinner or titillating fly as it comes boldly down the current. This would explain some of the tremendous salmon fishing I've encountered just downstream from dams, weirs, and other in-stream obstructions which bring about unusual concentrations of migrating salmon. This works with trout, bass, and other gamefish—why not with salmon?

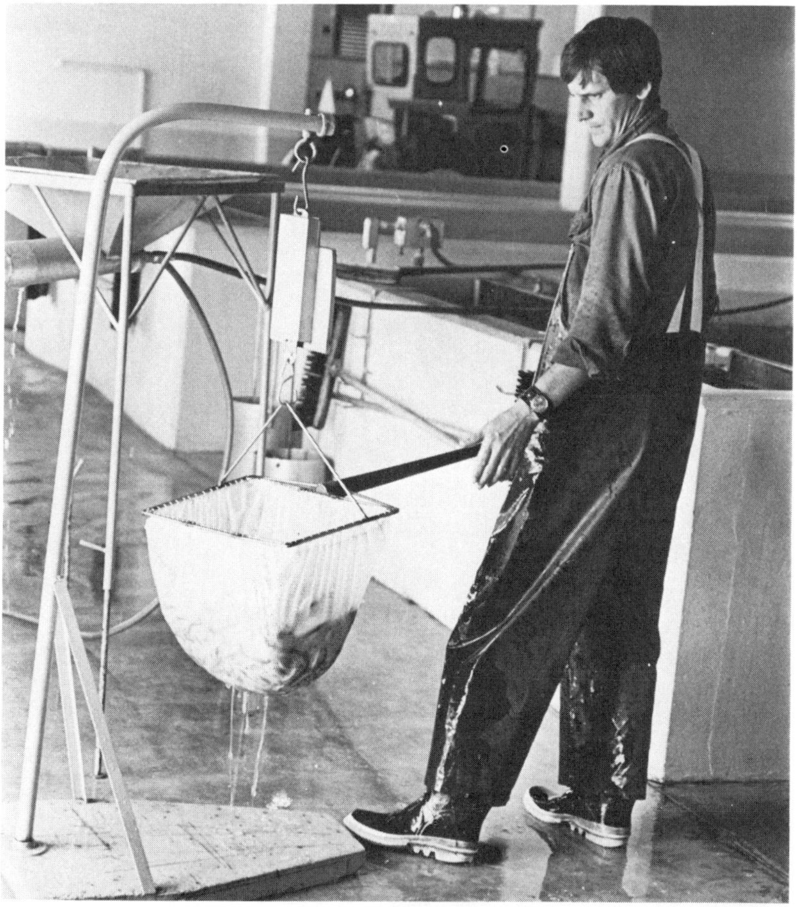

A state fish-hatchery worker weighs a netful of salmon smolts before stocking them in a holding pond. A large part of every license dollar is spent for restocking in the United States.

Where salmon hold in streams has befuddled more than one neophyte used to trout and smallmouth bass. Here's a rule of thumb which may help regardless of the stream you fish: Salmon use the stream only as a route of travel. They have no interest in feeding and choose their holding locations accordingly. Additionally, most migrating salmon travel at night, preferring to find some ideal spot just off the main current in which to rest while comfortable current sweeps over their bodies.

A lively column of young king salmon spill from a tile containing running water. Salmon states handle millions of young fish annually in support of public sportfishing.

On the several Great Lakes salmon rivers I have fished, the kings and cohos freshly out of Lakes Huron, Michigan, Erie, and Superior seem to have definite preferences in holding water. The outsides of horseshoe bends in the rivers are such spots, particularly where some type of obstruction breaks up the surge of the current. The obstacle may be as large as a pile of logs or an entire fallen tree, or as small as a single tree branch. The important thing, from the salmon's viewpoint, is finding a spot with enough current for creature comfort without forcing the fish to expend too much stored energy to remain in place.

I have seen big salmon, usually kings, porpoise regularly in broad daylight. The shipping canal at Sturgeon Bay, Wisconsin, which connects Green Bay with Lake Michigan, often is alive with leaping salmon during their September run into Strawberry Creek and a few other small creeks in the area. Huge kings on Michigan's Père Marquette and Betsie Rivers also break water with unnerving regularity, but no one seems to know why for certain. Some say they are merely playing, others say surfacing fish are males in combat. Perhaps the best explanation is one offered by fish expert Lee Kernen of the Wisconsin Department of Natural Resources: "If you hadn't had sex for four years and knew tonight was the night, you'd jump for joy too."

I remember one big king which taught me a lesson on Michigan's Père Marquette one October afternoon. I had been wading upstream from a steadily surfacing fish in shallow shoreline water, and promising myself I would move to cover it with my casts after working the water before me. Before I could move downstream, however, another fisherman came around a downstream bend and failed to see the steadily surfacing fish. He waded to the exact spot where the fish had been showing, and judging by his waders' depth in the pool the water there was less than 3 feet deep. He fished a while, then packed it in and moved beyond me to the pool above. Twenty minutes later the salmon was back in its original location, sending rollers over the green water. The point, of course, was that the fisherman had not only been fishing water too deep to catch the salmon he sought; he had actually spooked a fish from within easy casting distance of shore.

It is difficult for the newcomer to avoid placing too much emphasis on casting only to those stream salmon he can see. Most often this is a futile method when the fish are occasionally coming up top to thrash the water into foam or make the handsome symmetrical leaps for which the king salmon is noted. I have been as gullible as anyone in this pursuit and can honestly admit that not once when I cast to a surface-active salmon did I get an immediate strike. I have had some success, however, by using such surface shows as an aid in pinpointing the spots where salmon were holding in a particular pool. Whether the particular fish which struck my plug or bait was the one doing all the thrashing, I have no way of knowing. And besides, when you've hung a John Paul Jones fish—one that has only just begun to fight—who cares if there are others around?

Pacific salmon, particularly in the Great Lakes states where salmon are still relatively new, having been introduced in 1967, are subject to one of the controversial methods of capture yet devised by man. Call it snagging, foul-hooking, snatching, or jerking, it involves jerking a weighted treble hook along bottom where salmon are abundant until one or more of the barbs impales a fish and it is cranked ashore like some unwilling bale of hay. The fish may be hooked in the eye, the tail, the dorsal fin, or along its broad silvery side.

Some snaggers actually return home with the fish they have jerked, cleaning them for table use. But the strictly money-oriented jerks, like the legion of Michigan residents who are drawn to fall salmon runs as flies are drawn to carrion, care little for the many pounds of edible fish flesh they leave to rot on riverbanks in a day of snagging. Such individuals seek the twin skeins of salmon eggs in hen fish enroute to spawning grounds. One deft swipe with a sharp knife opens the salmon's belly from gills to anus, the egg skeins are ripped free, and the remainder of the carcass is left to stink on the river gravel or tossed back into the water for a slower deterioration.

A major force behind such brutal practice are the unscrupulous bait dealers in Detroit and other large Midwestern cities who pay cash for every pound of salmon eggs delivered by snaggers. As long as these egg markets exist there will be men willing to decimate Michigan's fall salmon runs for the money involved. Some of these men are true hard cases, and more than a few state conservation officers have been badly beaten by gangs of snaggers confronted with the evidence.

At least a few Michigan residents have had their fill. Jim Mattis, who along with his wife operates a small fishing resort on the lower Betsie River at Benzonia, takes time from his chores every autumn to patrol his stretch of the river. Some jerks leave quietly, fearing the law. Others, as Mattis has put it, require a bit more encouragement.

"Every fall for a few years we had a party of men in here when the salmon were running we got to know as the New York Boys. They had snagging down to a science. If they had put the effort into fishing fair they did into snagging, they'd have caught all the fish they wanted.

"One day my son, who's pretty big for his age and doesn't take much guff, followed a snagger downstream a little bit, my son on one side of the river, the jerk on the other. Every time the jerk would cast his snag hook into the water my son would intentionally snag it with his own hook, pull it out of the water and cut it off. When he finally got the message that my son wasn't going to let him snag here, he left."

Mattis has made his feelings known to the area's state conservation officer, but to little avail.

"Hell, he's off on Sunday and won't answer calls, so I suggested the state appoint a few local residents as deputies to patrol certain sections of the river. They wouldn't be recognized by the snaggers and could issue citations all up and down the river. So far the state hasn't acted on our suggestion, though."

Most states where salmon runs occur permit at least some snagging on designated sections of salmon rivers, giving the reason that the fish are going to die anyway and might as well be put to use. I remain adamant in the belief, however, that the overall volume of jerking would be considerably reduced if the downstate egg markets were put out of business through vigorous law enforcement and judicial followup.

ATLANTIC SALMON

Sportfishermen the world over have in common the belief that the tougher a particular fish is to catch, the higher its esteem among its followers. This undoubtedly is the case with the Atlantic salmon.

Kicking a salmon ashore is an accepted method of beaching the catch. Just be sure the fish is totally spent before trying it.

The fish is on its side and obviously ready for landing. Gilling is still a risky way to capture a large fish, however.

On many waters where it occurs in America and Canada, the Atlantic may be pursued with fly tackle only, and this only serves to make the task of bringing fish to net more difficult. Just imagine attempting to subdue a 20-pound leaping salmon on a 12-foot leader tipped with a diminutive No. 16 dry fly. Kind of like pass-shooting doves with a .22 rifle, and long odds indeed.

There is a great deal to set the Atlantic salmon apart from its Pacific Ocean relatives. Pacific salmon are, by and large, much easier to catch, and Atlantics may spawn three or more times in their lifetime, while Pacific fish spawn but once before dying. Pacific salmon enter their spawning streams in autumn, by and large, while Atlantics may move from salt to fresh water as early in the year as May or June, providing a summer run of big fish. Pacific species spawn in October and November and then die, while Atlantic fish spawn in early fall, then spend the remainder of the winter under stream ice before moving back down to the sea with the first flooding rain of spring. And, perhaps as a reward for the angler who travels the miles and spends the weeks seeking them, Atlantics are considered much better leapers than their Pacific relatives.

Hen salmon produce about 750 eggs per pound of body weight, fanning shallow beds in headwater stream gravel. Three or more redds may be created, one beside the other, and each time eggs are freed, the cock fish is alongside to cloud the water with milt and fertilize the eggs. Like Pacific salmon, newly hatched Atlantics absorb nutrition from the yolk sac attached to their bellies until the sac's contents are used up and the little salmon, now called alevins, are forced to leave the gravel and seek food in the stream. Growth among young alevins is much slower than among young domestic trout found in the same waters, and it may take the alevins-turned-smolts up to four years to reach the size and strength necessary for the long, tough journey down to the sea.

Once in the North Atlantic, however, the smolts travel amazing distances (up to 2,500 miles one way) to vast feeding areas where food is plentiful and rates of growth are rapid. Just when a particular salmon returns to its home stream for the first time depends on its strain. Some fish, called grilse, average three to five years of age and weigh about 4 pounds on their return to fresh water. Two-year-old adults weighing up to 12 or so pounds make up another age class. The largest Atlantics commonly found in spawning streams are adults five or six years old and weighing between 18 and 30 pounds. A fourth age class, fish that have spent up to six winters in the ocean, contains salmon weighing up to 45 or 50 pounds. These largest of Atlantics are most commonly found in the waters of Norway, and this country holds the present world record, a specimen weighing 79½ pounds.

But before you decide to fish only those rivers containing the largest, and therefore the oldest, Atlantics, you should know one fact which may send you back to angling for bullheads in the mud creek nearest your home: The longer these fish spend in the ocean before first returning to spawn, the less inclined they are to take a fly in the river or stream. It follows, then, that grilse, or single-year fish, are taken most readily by flyfishermen on waters with a run of grilse. The larger the salmon, the less inclined it is to suck in a wet fly or rise to a dry. Like Pacific salmon, Atlantics newly arrived in parent streams are more inclined to succumb to a well-placed fly than fish which have been in fresh water a few weeks. This may be because sea-bright fish are a bit reluctant to give in to instinct and stop all active feeding while away from the sea.

Why, then, will every third, or fifth or tenth, salmon take a fly? We can only surmise that something in the salmon's gray matter responds to irritation, annoyance, perhaps some shadowy recollection of its predatory instincts in the ocean. We do know that a salmon holding in a stream is most likely to take that fly the *first* time it is brought to his attention, and the chances for a take on subsequent drifts are reduced unless and until the fly is changed by size or color, or perhaps the presentation is a bit different. All of this is made much more frustrating, of course, because the fish is large, the water is clear and often shallow, and the fisherman very often sees the fish he casts over and therefore, I suspect, is tempted to throw stones at it, if only to receive the satisfaction of finally seeing it move.

There are theories and methods in common use, of course, that supposedly help lower the odds against the fisherman. Some claim that a cast diagonally upstream from the fish, with the rod tip kept pointed at the fly as it dead-drifts over the lie, is most effective. Yet not a mile downstream you'll hear another successful angler claim that a "worked" fly, one which is given a little life by minute twitches of the rod tip, is the best way to entice reluctant salmon. Among the most popular wet-fly patterns are the Muddler Minnow, Jock Scott, Silver Doctor, Black Dose, and Miller.

When streams are low and the water is especially clear, dry-fly fishing for Atlantics is at its most productive. The lower the water level, by and large, the smaller the fly, either in overall size or amount of bulk. Hair-bodied flies which ride high on stiff hackles are popular, but gossamerlike skaters and spiders also take many low-water fish. The Royal Coachman and white Wulff, the latter created by noted salmon flyfisherman Lee Wulff, can be very productive. Hook size depends for the most part on water level. Dries can range in size from No. 4 to No. 18, the thinking being that the more reluctant the fish, the smaller the fly. Unlike wet flies and streamers, which are most productive on cold, rising water, dries are best fished from middle through late summer, when salmon streams are low and in pool.

The *hitched* wet fly is a change in both the way the fly is rigged and the way it is fished. Hitching entails tying the fly to the leader as usual, then taking two half-hitches around the shank behind the eye of the hook. If the river is running from right to left as the angler faces it, the hitches should be on the left-hand side of the fly's head. If the current runs from left to right, the hitches should be on the fly's right side. This rigging causes the wet fly to rise to the surface film and make a V-shaped wake when retrieved and is often more attractive to the fish than the same fly would be when fished completely submerged. The hitched fly rides with the hook point facing downstream and is usually taken in a wide swirl, much like a dry is taken. Take care to wait those few important seconds after the swirl, however; depending on pure reflex when that swirl appears very often pulls the fly away before it is in the salmon's mouth. This is a very exciting way to fish for salmon.

Although the habitat of the Atlantic salmon has shrunk almost completely out of the rivers of New England and is now concentrated in Canada's Atlantic provinces and parts of northern Europe and Asia, there is reason to believe present salmon waters will remain at least reasonably stable. Much of the land bordering today's fine salmon rivers is either privately owned and coveted, or leased by wealthy fishermen no less careful about its conservation, and this bodes well for the future of the sport. Those waters available to the average fisherman require expenses ranging from $1,600 to $5,000 for a week or two of high-quality fishing; this price includes air transportation, lodging, stream fees, guides, and licenses.

And once on the stream, the visiting fisherman has no guarantee the salmon will cooperate. High stream flow may require a week or more to subside; cold weather may make reluctant fish even more close-mouthed. On some waters, one rise a day is about all an angler can expect. All of this keeps fishing pressure within reason.

In addition, commercial netting of the salmon's traditional feeding grounds off Greenland is being slowly phased out by the Danish fishing fleet, the last holdout in an international agreement to preserve this fine gamefish.

Baseball great Ted Williams, the sport's last .400 hitter during his nineteen-year tenure with the Boston Red Sox, splits his fishing year between Atlantic salmon on New Brunswick's Miramichi River and tarpon and bonefish in the Florida Keys around Islamorada. A dedicated flyfisherman, Williams says he catches between 80 and 120 salmon a year from the Miramichi. The fish range from grilse weighing 3 pounds to three-year-olds scaling 14 pounds and more, all on flies he ties himself.

"There are several patterns I favor," he told me not long ago. "The No. 1 Conrad tied all black with a yellow tail is real good, and so is something called the Happy Hooker, which is my own design. I use a double No. 8 or 10 hook on the Butterfly streamer wing, which catches a lot of salmon for me." Williams fishes a private stretch of the Miramichi off limits to anyone not a part of the river's lease agreement.

As this is written, a five-year-old program in Michigan may make high-quality Atlantic salmon fishing available to the average fisherman with only a weekend to spend. If some problems are solved, rivers mouthing in Lakes Michigan, Huron, and Superior may one day support major summer runs of these fine aerial battlers.

In the spring of 1972, a fleet of four tank trucks and one support vehicle departed Michigan for the Domtar Salmon Center in eastern Quebec. Several thousand salmon smolts had been jointly purchased by the Michigan Department of Natural Resources and the Michigan United Conservation Clubs. Rivers on the state's east and west sides were to receive the smolts, while adult breeder fish went to the Wolf Lake hatchery at Kalamazoo. Ten thousand of the little Atlantics went into the Au Sable River upstream from Oscoda to Foote Dam, and another 10,000 went into the Boyne River between Lake Charlevoix and the dam 3 miles upstream.

A year later, Michigan acquired two more strains of the still-experimental Atlantics. Vermont sent eyed salmon eggs in 1975 in exchange for steelhead eggs, and Sweden sent a gift of eggs from its Gullspang salmon strain, native to Sweden's Lake Vänern. Gullspangs, it is hoped, will provide the largest adult salmon, because their parent water produces Atlantics up to 66 pounds.

Jim Copeland, hatchery manager at Wolf Lake, said he hopes the Atlantics will provide a summer run of fish. "We wanted a large salmonid that would be available to stream fishermen in midsummer, and if we can solve some problems, the Atlantic should be that fish."

The problems Copeland mentioned are considerable and narrow down to keeping the adult salmon alive long enough to spawn a second time. To date, three-year-old spawners returning to the Boyne and Au Sable suffer a mortality rate of nearly 70 percent after entering the stream. The once-silvery fish turn a dark, drab olive color and die.

Research has shown that the Atlantic is particularly susceptible to furunculosis, a disease resulting from contact with a bacteria common to Michigan waters. Brown trout also contract the disease, and since Wolf Lake also handles brown trout, care must be taken to keep the two systems apart. To combat the disease, antibiotics are coated on the hatchery salmon's high-fat food pellets.

Large, bright baits, such as spinners, wobbling plugs, and spoons, can be deadly for big salmon when fished in good holding water. This coho fell for a homemade spinner with a No. 5 Colorado blade.

Another and perhaps more important threat to the Great Lakes' Atlantic salmon program is the pollution common to both Lakes Huron and Michigan. Pesticides and PCBs (polychlorinated biphenyls) are thought to prevent salmon from spawning a second time; the same chemicals are also believed to be responsible for the two lakes' massive decline in natural lake-trout reproduction. Several states bordering the two lakes are now demanding laws designed to prevent the further introduction of these harmful pollutants into interstate waters.

There are some meager results from past Atlantic stocking programs, however. As of this writing, the top Atlantic taken from the mouth of the Boyne River weighed a hefty 16 pounds, 3 ounces. Michigan's current state-record Atlantic, taken from the mouth of the Au Sable by Elmer Caswell of Oscoda, weighed 20 pounds, 1 ounce, and taped 39 inches long. Fishermen may angle for Au Sable salmon with spinning gear if they wish, but the Boyne River's 3 miles of Atlantic-salmon water is closed to all but flyfishing, and all salmon must be returned unharmed to the water. These regulations should remain unchanged until Michigan solves its pollution problems and the new salmon becomes established in more rivers.

So the Atlantic salmon remains a very *special* fish, even in its native waters of Canada and Scandinavia. It is tough to catch, a wonderful adversary on hook and line, and unless problems are solved in the Great Lakes, too expensive a bargain ever to be overfished. And this is as it should be.

STEELHEAD

The first steelhead trout I ever saw went by so fast I couldn't identify it. A fisherman two pools upstream from my spot on Michigan's Little Manistee River had hooked the fish, which he later estimated to weigh 8 pounds, and managed to keep it on just long enough for the fish to start the flashing, jumping downstream run for which the steelie is so famous.

By the time the fish had passed me, it had already broken off but continued to leap completely out of the water in an attempt to dislodge the hook. In a few seconds it had tail-walked around a bend in the stream and was gone. The fisherman reeled up his now-slack line (a bit dejectedly, I thought), and waded ashore to recoup.

Wherever it is found and however it is caught, the steelhead draws the fisherman's raves. Many consider this big, overgrown rainbow trout to be fresh water's finest fighting fish—an opinion I am close to sharing.

Salmo gairdneri, also called steelie and roaming rainbow, is in its original state an anadromous fish, one which migrates up freshwater streams from the ocean to spawn. Its original range lies along the northeastern and northwestern U.S.

coasts and into Canada on both the Pacific and Atlantic shores, and in Alaska. Through greatly expanded fish management and research projects on the Great Lakes, however, Midwestern anglers may today find blue-ribbon steelhead fishing in dozens of rivers and streams in Michigan, Minnesota, Wisconsin, and even Illinois and Indiana.

The steelhead, although actually just one strain of the common rainbow trout, reaches sizes far greater than its bright-hued and smaller cousins. First-year stream steelhead may average only 1½ to 2 pounds, while mature fish (four years or older) may reach weights upwards of 30 pounds. Most fish caught by anglers, however, will weigh somewhere between 5 and 15 pounds.

Virtually all of this weight is gained during the fish's years in big water, be it the ocean or one of the Great Lakes. Here they eat baitfish such as smelt, alewives, squid, and the fry of other gamefish species. So plentiful is the food supply in Lakes Michigan and Huron, for example, that steelhead at the end of their third year in the big water may have gained 20 pounds and gone from 6-inch smolts to fish of 30 or more inches.

Unlike the domestic rainbow, steelhead seldom obtain the bright-red lateral coloration found in trout which spend all their lives in streams and rivers. Wherever found, the steelhead's colors are steel-gray along the dorsal side from snout to tail. The rainbowlike black spots are found only on the steel's tailfin, and the gray color fades to a silver-white on the ventral side. Although so-called "green" fish, those freshly entering spawning streams from lake or ocean, are somewhat lighter than described, they lose this light shade quickly as they pass time in the stream.

Steelhead runs, or migrations, occur twice annually on most streams, although actual spawning occurs only in spring. Fish biologists do not know specifically why fall runs occur. Some suggest the fish follow spawning salmon to feed on the salmon's eggs, while other experts say the steelhead are merely obedient to a strong urge to enter their native streams and move upstream. Whatever the reason for the spring and fall movements, such runs make the fish available to the angler.

In the Great Lakes states, steelies usually enter the rivers to spawn in early to mid-April, depending upon water temperature. If the water reaches the upper 30s, steelies will be drawn from their staging area just off the river mouths and into the stream. The run continues in stops and starts if the weather and temperature vacillate, with those fish already well upstream holding in the deepest pools while the fish nearer the river mouths drop back until a warming trend occurs.

I have caught Michigan steelhead as early as the first weekend in March when the water temperature read a chilling 33°. The fickle Michigan spring had stalled, plunging the temperature and halting all movement by the steelhead. I had to work twice as hard for my fish that day, although we managed to coax fish of 6 and 11 pounds to nibble a spawn bait near bottom in 12 feet of water on the Betsie River.

In the upper Midwest, fishermen can expect spring steelheading to reach a peak when water temperatures reach 41° or 42°. This optimum temperature seems to stimulate the greatest number of migrating fish to move in the stream, and steelhead are known to strike most readily during rising water conditions. Once on the spawning beds or drifting back downstream following the spawn, the fish become less and less interested in feeding, apparently content to seek out lake or ocean to rest after the rigors of reproduction.

Fall runs of steelhead occur in the Great Lakes beginning in early October, with the greatest number of fish in the streams in late October and November, and this is when anglers using artificial baits do best. Fall-run fish are usually far more willing to chase and strike a passing lure than are spring steelies, and have been known to send a man home with a two-piece rod that came to the stream in a one-piece condition. Sometimes, as I witnessed on Michigan's Au Sable River in the fall of 1975, the fisherman breaks the rod himself.

A young fisherman directly across the river from me had hooked and lost three consecutive steelhead in forty-five minutes, so when the fourth fish hit his spinner he seemed to play it with extra care.

The steelie, a fish of about 10 pounds, first jumped some 20 yards downstream from the angler who loosened his drag

Dworshak dam provides a backdrop for Dworshak National Fish Hatchery at the confluence of the North Fork of the Clearwater River, and the Clearwater itself. This is the world's largest steelhead trout hatchery. Courtesy U.S. Fish & Wildlife Service.

accordingly. The second water-clearing jump was 10 yards farther away, and the third yet another 20 yards downstream. The fish then surfaced and rolled on the weakened line, and it parted with a loud pop. The angler then slowly waded back to shore, broke his fishing rod over one knee, tossed it far out into the river, and stalked back to his car. Score it Steelhead 4, Angler 0.

Some fish remain in the rivers and streams all winter, and others prefer the stream life in the summer. These fish do provide some off-season angling, but the steelheading on most Midwestern waters doesn't get serious until spring or fall, although a few hardcore anglers do fish all winter where open water is available.

Since the fish must pass through all of the stream between lake or ocean and the spawning beds, fishermen might be tempted to believe they can find fish virtually anywhere in the stream once a run is on, but this mistaken belief has sent hundreds of novice steelheaders home with nothing more than damp waders and no fish. True, steelhead must pass through the entire stream downstream from their destination, but most in-stream movement is made at night; daylight hours are spent in suitable pools and deep runs where the fish rest and feed, called holding water. So the secret is to know where to look for the fish, then how to fish it successfully.

Steelhead streams contain runs and pools which draw fish every year. Often the only way fishermen new to the stream can locate such spots is to inquire at local bait shops or look for knots of fishermen concentrating on certain areas on the stream, because there is seldom anything visible about the holding areas to set them apart from nearby pools and riffles devoid of fish. I know of one such spot less than 100 yards downstream from a well-traveled bridge on Michigan's Au Sable. No doubt hundreds of anglers drive over the bridge daily when the run is on, but judging by the sparsity of anglers fishing the pool, very few are aware the hotspot is there.

Some streams are so narrow and clear that steelhead can be seen from shore. This calls for extremely cautious fishing, sometimes including a kneeling approach to the stream and casting from all fours. Wisconsin steelheaders fishing the tiny creeks feeding Green Bay and Lake Michigan face these extra problems every spring and fall on such small, brushy streams as Heines Creek south of Bailey's Harbor, Hibbard's Creek just north of Jacksonport, and Stoney Creek on the Door County line in the Kewaunee District. The dilemma facing devotees of such mini-waters is the need for light lines to avoid spooking fish, and the need for enough heft in their equipment to contain wildly fighting fish in small-water, brushy conditions. It should be added that many Wisconsin steelheaders concentrate around stream mouths where there is open water to play big rainbows (they are seldom called steelhead in the Badger State) and the odd brown that hits spawn baits meant for steelies.

Michigan's lovely Platte River, which meets Lake Michigan near the town of Beulah in Benzie County, is exceptionally crystalline and flows over light-colored sand. Fish are quite easily spotted by anglers wading the river's hard-packed sand bottom, and the sport takes on the aspects of hunting as the quarry is spotted, a stalk planned, and a careful cast made. Even the deepest of the Platte's pools offer good visibility, so extreme care must be the byword or the wary steelhead will detect the angler and dart away. The Platte is typical of many steelhead rivers in that it affords the fish little protection through natural cover, and fishermen seek their quarry near whatever objects exist in suitable pools and runs—submerged logs, rocks, low-level dams, and gravel beds. The fish hold beside or just downstream from such objects and can be seen as dark shapes in position near the cover.

Sometimes hunting the fish can be as much of a challenge as catching them. One morning on the Little Manistee River I waded around the bend to discover two anglers working as a team. One had climbed a sizable streamside tree and was perched on a limb overhanging the water. From his overhead position he had spotted a pair of spawning steelies and had pointed out their position to his friend, who got into position to make a good cast. When one angler had caught a fish, the two changed positions some distance upstream where another gravel bed was likely to contain at least a few spawning fish.

Spawning steelhead—and this means strictly spring fish—can very often be seen in the stream because of the shallow water in which their redds, or spawning beds, are made. Hen (female) steelies seek out clean gravel beds washed by 1 to 3 feet of current. She uses her strong, wide tail to sweep out a shallow depression in the gravel, all the while closely attended by one or more male fish eager to fertilize her eggs. Very often the male fish are smaller than the female, and finding two or more males attending one female can mean a bonanza opportunity for the watchful steelheader. Competition is high among such male fish, and careful casting can sometimes result in two fish taken from the same spot, provided a hooked fish's antics don't startle the female and her escorts off the gravel bed.

Clearwater-spawned steelhead is stripped of its eggs during the annual April egg-taking period. Eggs are then mixed with male's milt, fertilizing them and continuing the cycle. Spawned-out adult fish are returned to the river. Courtesy U.S. Fish & Wildlife Service.

The most productive baits, whether artificial or prepared, depend on the type of tackle being used and the whims of the fish themselves. It is a fair statement that steelhead will, at one time or another, mouth virtually anything an angler sees fit to toss into the water, and at no time is this more true than during the spring spawn.

Like the largemouth bass that vigorously attacks anything which enters its spawning bed, the hen steelhead will mouth and remove virtually any object which drifts into her redd. Steelhead have been known to strike such unlikely objects as twigs, rolling pebbles, and cigarette butts which came to rest in or near the spawning bed. Noticing this, fishermen soon learned they could bury a hook in almost any easily cast object, drift it into the spawning area, and anticipate strikes from the preoccupied fish.

Among the unusual baits used for spawning steelhead, particularly in the northeastern states, are tiny marshmallows, half-inch tassle balls found on old-fashioned curtains, small sponges cut into squares, and even tiny bits of wallpaper-cleaning compound molded around a No. 6 hook. As unlikely as it sounds, hen steelies have been taken on these baits because of their determination to keep all foreign objects out of the spawning redd. But, again like bass, hen steelhead only mouth baits at this time, retaining them in their lips only long enough to move a short distance downstream from the nest before spitting them out, so a fast, sharp strike is necessary to hook these spawners.

A longtime favorite for stream-running steelhead in both spring and fall is salmon eggs, fished either singly or in clusters within 6 inches of bottom. This is drift fishing, and the tackle must be chosen accordingly.

The drift fisherman travels the stream until he locates good holding water, either a deep, slick run of fast water or a deep riffle with plentiful side pockets of water shielded by logs or other objects. This is where the migrating steelhead pause during daylight hours to rest and perhaps feed a little as food is available. The fisherman's job is to make his spawn bait as available as possible to the greatest number of fish.

There are two methods of preparing clusters of eggs. In the first, fresh, single eggs are rolled in borax, which keeps them fresh and easier to handle, and then five or more eggs are grouped inside 2-inch squares of fine mesh, such as from an old pair of women's nylon hose. The square is shaped into a little sac around the eggs and tied shut with strong thread. The second method requires drying an entire skein of salmon eggs, just as they come out of a fresh-caught salmon. The skein is air-dried overnight and cut lengthwise into strips, then cut again into 1-inch cubes of about six to eight eggs each. These can then be either rolled in borax or used immediately. The secret is to include a bit of the skein's "skin" with each cube to help keep the cluster in one piece on the hook.

Regardless of how you prepare your spawn bait, the most important requirement is consistently getting the bait within 6 inches of bottom. With few exceptions, running steelhead will seldom move very far for a bait, and this is particularly true in early spring when stream temperature is marginal and the fish are lethargic.

Perhaps the most popular rigging for drift-fishing spawn calls for a three-way swivel. One end of the swivel leads to the main fishing line, and a second leads to 18 to 24 inches of strong monofilament (15-to-20-pound test) to which is clinch-knotted a No. 6 heavy-duty hook. I prefer that the hook have a short shank with one or two barbs; this small, strong hook is easily hidden inside an egg cluster, and the barbs help anchor the cluster during repeated casting. If the hooks you use feature a turned-up or turned-down eye, then you should use the turle knot.

To the third end of the swivel is tied an 8-inch length of 6-pound-test monofilament, which carries the lead weight necessary to keep the rig drifting near bottom. Many steelheaders, particularly in the Far West, tie a few inches of surgical rubber tubing to their line. Into this narrow tubing is thrust the desired weight of pencil-shaped lead sinker, the idea being that the lead, if fouled on bottom rocks or logs, will pull out of the tubing while leaving the rest of the rig intact. A method in wide use on Great Lakes rivers simplifies the weight problem a bit and calls for the addition of two or more split shot to the third dropper line. Since the weight dropper line is only 6-pound-test, it usually breaks off if snagged and need only be replaced if lost to snags. And if you use the new type of split shot with small lead "wings," which permit the shot to be opened and closed as often as desired, weight can be added or subtracted as needed according to the water conditions.

A bait which bridges the gap between real salmon eggs and artificial lures is the Okie Drifter, really nothing more than a fake egg cluster made of hollow plastic. The Drifters, about the size and shape of an acorn, come in a variety of colors and have a small hole through which line is threaded. Michigan anglers, particularly on that state's eastern side, tie a two-way swivel on the end of their 12-pound monofilament line, adding one or more ½-ounce sliding barrel sinkers above the swivel. To the swivel's lower end is tied 18 inches of 20-pound leader material. The Drifter is threaded on this leader and a heavy No. 2 hook finishes the rig. This rigging puts the Drifter within a few inches of bottom, while the sliding barrel sinker helps avoid snags.

Both real egg clusters and Okie Drifters are cast diagonally upstream and permitted to sink deep and drift freely through holding water suspected to contain steelhead. Almost any type of standard fishing tackle—spinning, plugcasting, or fly—will do as long as the rod is long enough to keep the fishing line up off the water from rod tip to where the line enters the stream. This is important because steelhead take spawn baits and Drifters very gently; allowing slack line to touch the stream surface puts too much drag on the line and many "takes" by fish will go undetected.

If you're like me, Old Dumb Thumb, you will have to serve a steelheader's apprenticeship when fishing spawn or Drifters. I had to spend several cold, damp days thigh-deep in steelhead water before I learned to detect the difference between the bump-bump of my weighted rig bouncing along bottom, and the gentle tap of a taking fish. In fact, the first fish I ever hooked was quite accidental. I'd been casting-retrieving, casting-retrieving for an hour or so with no results and decided the pool was barren and I needed a smoke. I stopped fishing in mid-drift and began reeling rapidly, thinking I'd wade ashore, plop down against a tree trunk, and think dark thoughts about this steelheading business.

The line was still slack when a large, silvery fish bored a hole in the river directly in front of me and jumped. It fell back with a mighty splash and ran downstream, and only then did my line tighten and my rod come alive. But by that time I was so amazed to see an honest-to-God fish that I stood stock-still and let the fish get away on its next jump. If the experience hadn't been a complete success, it had at least given me a little confidence.

I think the bottom line of learning to detect and hook steelhead on spawn baits or Drifters is: Pay Attention. Fish these baits often enough and you'll soon learn how a taking fish feels. Some fish will move slightly away after gobbling the bait, and these are easier than most to detect, but 99

Dressed warmly against the cold, the author hefts a spring steelhead from Michigan's Platte River. The water temperature was 34 degrees, and the air was colder.

percent will merely mouth the bait without changing position. It's best to strike hard anytime you feel something that might be a fish. That way you can't go wrong.

A trick popular on the West Coast is the addition of a bit of bright fluorescent yarn just above the hook, with red, orange, and green predominating. The theory is that the few inches of colored yarn add just enough attraction to the spawn bait to get those reluctant steelhead to strike. Some steelheaders swear by this method of attracting fish, but it's mostly a West Coast idea and seldom seen in the Great Lakes.

Wobbling and diving-type plugs are popular among both waders and boat fishermen anywhere steelhead exist. Plugs of the Tad Polly, U20 Flatfish, Lazy Ike Jawbreaker, and other similar patterns all catch their share of fish and are usually "hung" in the current rather than cast and retrieved. The fisherman using plugs stations himself on the downstream edge of riffles and drops his plug into the water, paying out line until the plug is positioned at the head of the pool. Here the reel is switched into the forward position and the plug is permitted to hang in the current, boring deep and wobbling. If no strike occurs, a few more feet of line are payed out from the reel and the plug is again wobbled in the current. The system continues until a fish strikes or the entire pool is covered. The method of lowering a plug through holding water in stages is designed to locate the plug as close as possible to holding fish.

Overall plug size and action are the most important considerations, but color does play a role. In dingy water, use bright colors of red, chartreuse, and all white. In shallow, clear water I prefer silver or silver-and-blue plugs. Black can be deadly in muddy water.

Large-bladed spinners and spoons take many steelhead every year, particularly in large, heavy streams. Spinners of the No. 5 Mepps type are excellent, as they can be cast upstream and retrieved with the current. Several steelhead addicts I know assemble their own large spinners with dropper-type blades, red bead bodies, and hefty treble hooks. This can save considerable cash when fishing snag-filled waters—and waters containing 20-pound steelhead which have a nasty habit of breaking off while still festooned with your spinner. Spoons should measure from 1 to 3 inches long, be constructed of heavy-gauge metal, and be highly polished.

Blue, silver-blue, red, and all silver are preferred colors, and these too are cast diagonally upstream and retrieved slowly.

Let's spend a moment on my favorite steelhead topic: the strike. Do not be fooled into thinking that steelies take plugs and spinners as lightly as they gobble spawn baits. I know of no studies on exactly how many pounds of force a steelhead expends when it hits a plug, so I can only estimate that it is in the neighborhood of a freight train hitting a brick wall. Whether out of hunger or anger (or just for the hell of it), whatever moves a steelie to pursue and catch a lure also moves the fish to destroy it at the same time. In fact a friend of mine who owned a tackle shop in Ludington, near the Pentwater and Père Marquette Rivers, used to display a peck basket in his store window. The basket was full of all types of steelhead plugs, each of them rendered useless by the fish. Trebles had been straightened or pulled completely out, the plugs' rear halves were missing, or the diving plates on the front of the plugs had been bitten in two. There is one advantage to such tremendous strikes, however: The fish usually hook themselves, leaving the angler only to hang on for dear life while trying to get his heart restarted.

There are those in the Brotherhood of Fishermen and Other Questionable Types who consider the steelhead's sport a thing of beauty only for the fly rod. To take steelies any other way is something less than God intended, and having tried this toughest of angling methods I am hard pressed to disagree.

Gary Schnicke, a regional-fishery biologist stationed near Mio, Michigan, on the Au Sable River, holds the flyfisherman's art above all others and claims that spring-run steelhead respond to a well-presented fly better than to any other type of bait or lure. Schnicke, at my request, listed his preferred steelhead patterns, and these pretty well reflect those patterns used elsewhere on Michigan's deservedly acclaimed rivers and streams.

The Spring's Wiggler, a buggy-looking nymph tied on No. 4 to No. 8 hooks, was originated by Muskegon fly-tier Ron Spring. The pattern's original intent was merely to imitate any of the buggy-looking nymphs found in steelhead water, but the pattern became so popular on both the Père Marquette and Au Sable Rivers that today the nymph is said to imitate the nymphal stage of a large burrowing mayfly found in those waters. Spring says he now ties the fly in a number of color variations, including white, black, gray, and fox squirrel and bucktail.

Another of Schnicke's favorite patterns is the Père Marquette Special, a large, gaudy wet fly tied in bright orange or red body with silver ribbing and red-yellow wing and tail.

A streamer simply called the Blue Fly is at its best when the waters are slightly high and discolored, such as one might find in spring. The fly's body is all silver wrapping with a blue-and-white polar-bear hairwing and a wisp of red bucktail at the rear. This pattern is sometimes tied with a plain blue wing and can be a very hot lure under high-water conditions. Other murky-water streamers, tied on No. 2 or No. 4 4XL hooks, also produce their share of fish when dressed in all-white, yellow, or all-blue.

Other patterns I have found useful at one time or another include the Babine Special, Royal Coachman Wet, Thor, Muddler Streamer, and Skunk. Some scaled-down salmon streamers also produce, such as the Silver Abbey, Squirrel Doctor, Copper Killer, and Black Dose.

The problem of getting the fly down to fish level isn't as great as it used to be, thanks to the introduction of high-density sinking-tip and full-sinking lines. For extreme situations, lead-core fly lines are available which sink through even the heaviest current, although they are sometimes heavy enough on the pickup to require heavier fly rods.

On the West Coast, steelheaders who fish large, fast rivers favor the shooting head, a great aid to big-water flyfishermen which originated on the Klamath and Eel Rivers in the late forties. The shooting head consists of about 30 feet of weight-forward flyline with a loop spliced in at each end. The leader is attached to the forward loop, while the rear loop leads to a 75-foot section of 20-pound monofilament. The shooting head permits long casts with only a single backcast using the double-haul technique, and excellent sinking takes place if the head is made of a full-sinking or lead-core line. Fly lines

Hand-landing that big steelhead is romantic, but oh! that water is cold!

already made up in shooting heads are available at tackle shops catering to the steelheader on the West Coast.

Live-bait fishing for steelhead isn't often seen and is restricted to the use of mayfly larvae, called wigglers, and the infrequent use of worms or nightcrawlers. I have seen both baits fished on fly rods rigged with open-bail spinning reels filled with 6-to-8-pound monofilament line. Small hooks were used with only a few small split shot for weight, and the baits were allowed to drift with the current, usually on quite small waters such as Michigan's Little Manistee, the headwaters of the Platte, or Cherry Creek in the Upper Peninsula near Marquette.

A mistake often made by nonresident anglers trying for steelhead for the first time is using the same tackle, rigged in the same way, for steelhead that serves for catfish or bass back home. Steelies are caught on such gear occasionally, but these are the exceptions. Rod-and-reel combinations fine-tuned for, say, largemouth bass often won't do the job for these silvery bombshells of coldwater streams. If you plan to become a steelheader with any frequency, it's far better to gear up properly in the first place.

Open-bail spinning outfits are undoubtedly the most popular rigs for steelhead and therefore the most frequently seen tackle on the water, for the same reasons as for other freshwater fish: Spinning permits a wide variety of line tests, bait sizes, and casting distances, all with a minimum of effort from the chap on the back end of the rod. Some lures, such as spinners and spoons, weigh quite a bit and can be cast long distances with no trouble. But switch terminal gear to the fragile salmon eggs, and casting becomes more of a tossing or slinging motion. Spinning serves both requirements well.

There are two reasons why I advise buying the best spinning reel you can afford, and both deal with catching, as well as hooking, good fish. Quality reels contain high-grade drag systems, which are important when trying to slow or stop the screeching downstream run of a hefty hen steelie. The other is the basic reliable construction of good equipment, including double springing in the bail release system (in case one spring breaks on the water), a drag adjustment somewhere other than on top of the spool where it will invariably get in the way if you try to adjust drag while fighting a fish, and the ease with which one spool can be removed and replaced with another.

The spinning rod is at least as important a choice as the reel, because it has a couple of specialized chores to do. It must have a fairly soft tip to help you detect those super-light takes on spawn and Drifters, and it must be long enough (7–8 feet is optimum) to keep your line, from rod tip to water, above the surface. The butt section of the rod should be hefty enough to horse a heavy fish if the occasion arises, and the handle should be of quality cork and long enough to accommodate two hands for lobbing baits long distances and battling strong fish in heavy current.

Also important are the guides on that rod. Simple chromed steel guides will do, but don't pass up the Carboloy-coated guides which permit longer casts and longer line life. These special guides put less wear and tear on the line by reducing friction heat. The new graphite rods are quite nice, offering the same amount of power and guts as their fiberglass counterparts but requiring less muscle from the fisherman. Yet the graphite models available today cost several times what a comparable glass stick does, and last no longer when crunched in car doors.

What about line to put on that new outfit? Regardless of the strength of the line you choose, obtain the best-quality line available and make it limp enough to cast well yet stiff enough to withstand the thousand little shocks steelheading line is heir to. Line test depends on the type of water you fish and how long you want to play your fish. One angler I know, discouraged by the declining steelhead production in his hometown stream, exchanged heavier gear for 4-pound monofilament on an ultralight spinning outfit and at last report is catching (or at least hooking) as many fish as before. Using light line can be of help in teasing shy fish in heavily trafficked waters. As a rule, however, line chosen for spinning outfits varies between 8-pound and 17-pound test and is clear or clear-blue, rather than yellow or orange.

Plugcasting gear for steelhead is, in my view, really just a blowup of tackle used for muskie and big northern pike. The reel should be level-wind with a free-spool feature and adjustable drag. The rod should be at least 7 feet long and built similarly to the spinning rod already described. In fact, some anglers actually use heavy freshwater or light saltwater spinning rods when plugcasting for steelhead.

Rod length and reel quality are as essential when using plugcasting gear as when using spinning gear. The rod should be somewhat longer than 6 feet—say between 6½ and 7½ feet—with a soft tip and plenty of heft in the lower section. The reel should be free-spool and capable of tossing ¼-ounce weights at least 30 yards.

Fishing tackle for steelheading, regardless of its type, should be one thing above all else: rugged. Steelhead are found in fast, twisting, rock-studded streams which give rod, reel, and line a most sincere field test. Add this to the often overpowering strength and agility of these silvery torpedoes, and you quickly appreciate the need for tackle which will serve hour after hour and week after week with only minor repairs, line changes, and the usual care.

Fortunately, today's tackle market offers excellent quality tackle which will stand up to day-in and day-out steelheading on even the most rugged streams and rivers. There are, for example, single-action fly reels which offer floating-disc-brake systems so designed that they simply will not freeze up in the middle of the run of a big fish. The manufacturers have assembled the drag so that heat caused by extended use of the reel drag will not expend the brakes and cause tackle failure.

For plugcasters, today's market has made available level-wind casting reels with built-in casting drags, side-mounted star drags which may be safely adjusted while fighting a fish, and even a rugged specialized model which permits the drag to work only when the twin crank handles are released. Others offer high-speed operation; this is welcome when working weighted spoons or spinners in deep, fast water where a rapid pickup is needed to keep the lure from hanging up on bottom. These reels, very popular among largemouth-bass fishermen, have a spool-revolution-to-crank ratio of 4.7 : 1 and handle most monofilament casting lines very adequately.

Stan Lievense, a Michigan fishery biologist and tourist information officer for over thirty years, is a firm believer in using only rugged fishing tackle for steelhead, and considering Stan's rather unusual approach to enticing and landing his fish, special tackle is needed.

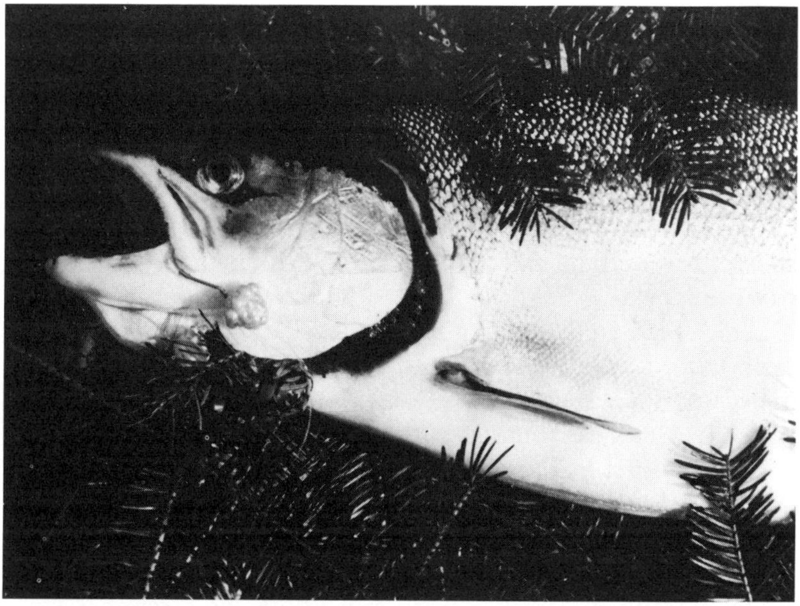

The Okie Drifter, a hollow molded-plastic bait designed to resemble an egg cluster, is one of several odd but productive steelhead baits.

To reach fish level in fast streams—and that means bottom—Lievense ties in a 2½-foot section of braided stainless-steel wire behind a similar length of leader material.

"This will get you down where the fish should be," he says. "The only problem with this method is the wire. It is rather easily crimped if you happen to lay a cast across a rock or a log."

Lievense has also developed steelhead lures, some of which are being marketed today. A flyfishing innovation he designed calls for a tiny plastic lip to be tied in at the hook's eye so that it rides below the eye, in much the same manner as diving lips on crankbaits used for bass. Lievense claims a bright streamer so equipped actually wiggles when suspended in stream current, permitting him to "stage" his wiggle fly down through a run of fast water in much the same manner as the plugcaster works his plug.

Another bait Lievense created, which is today available under the trade name Creek Chub Cheekie, is a lead-bodied spinning lure weighing ¼ ounce with the special feature of remaining within 6 inches of bottom during retrieve through virtually any type of current. The bait carries a single droplet spinner in front, followed by a bright-painted lead body, and a large treble hook dressed in white nylon. I've caught fish on this bait while using spinning gear and was impressed with the manner in which it rode over and around rocks while hanging near bottom in heavy current. I should think the same type of bait would be effective for salmon, domestic trout, and walleye.

Besides the basic tools of rod and reel and lures, virtually all experienced steelheaders outfit themselves with a minimum of accessories which aid the sport, either in finding the fish or in the angler's personal comfort.

Not the least of these is a good set of polarized sunglasses, the better kind which reduces or eliminates glare and thereby reduces eyestrain and permits the fisherman to see through the stream's surface. Seldom is this more important than when wading unfamiliar waters or when the stream is clear enough to permit individual fish to be seen. Many of the streams I fish for steelies are what I call "blackwaters." They are streams which course over black or dark-colored bottom sediment and which are virtually impossible to navigate safely without the aid of good glasses. One moment the sun is out and the stream bottom can be seen in great detail; the next moment the sun is behind a cloud and all the angler without sunglasses sees is dark water in which to wade.

Even the clearest streams can be more productive when polarized sunglasses are used. Fishing companion Pete Fusco and I visited Michigan's Platte River early one spring when the steelhead run was on "hold" because of a severe temperature drop. None of the usual fishing tactics worked, and we were forced to hunt individual fish, then make careful casts and hope. Fusco had no glasses and I did, and by lunch I had seen five fish and caught three while the only fish Fusco had seen thrashed widly out of his path after almost being stepped upon by the wading angler.

A good set of hip boots and/or chest waders is a must because the steelheader must go to the fish, and this means getting into the water within reach of holding spots. Both hip boots and chest-high waders have their place, but if you must choose between the two, buy the best pair of chest waders you can find. They will keep you dry in the shallows, yet handle water depths to within a few inches of your armpits. If you can afford two pair and plan to fish summer and winter, by all means purchase one pair of insulated waders and one pair of shells. Whichever you purchase, however, insist that they include deeply cleated soles and enough roominess to allow for those sprints down the shoreline to follow running fish before they take you into the backing. The best guarantee you can expect with even the best waders and hip boots is the manufacturer's assurance that they won't crack or peel because of ozone, so don't store them crumpled in a heap near your lawn mower; gasoline fumes have been known to eat holes in good waders.

Whether to carry a landing net is often a matter of personal choice and, to a lesser degree, dependent on the stream conditions. Many steelheaders prefer to tire a fish they plan to keep fully before bringing it close, then carefully moving into the shallows and literally kicking the exhausted fish ashore. Great Lakes steelheaders, however, seem to prefer to carry wide, deep-mesh landing nets built on aluminum frames; they hang them down the back of their waders. Many of the streams and rivers in the Midwest have brushy shorelines where beaching a fish is impractical, and the large nets come in handy. Steelhead may be gilled, but this often overstresses a fish and should not be done with fish intended for release.

The use of small, light boats and canoes on even small streams allows fishermen to hit a number of widely separated hotspots in a day's time, and unless you like to paddle or row more than I do, you'll want some sort of motor to get you there and back. Small aluminum V-bottom boats are comfortable for one or two occupants and have the added advantage of good maneuverability on winding streams. Johnboats are popular and can be pushed along nicely by outboards in the 2–4-horsepower class. Particularly popular on small Midwestern streams are canoes, both square-stern and double-end models. The lighter canoes, of fiberglass or aluminum, are easily propelled by electric trolling motors. I prefer fiberglass

A lone steelheader casts again and again to a slick of deep water. Repeated casting is a fact of life among avid steelhead fishermen.

construction because aluminum is so noisy when scraped. Fiberglass is also more easily repaired.

Warm clothing is, of course, a must for late-fall or early-spring steelheading, not to mention dependable raingear. I can't recall a day of spring fishing when the day offered anything better than low, leaden skies, intermittent rain and/or snow, and generally foul weather. But I also remember being surprised at how quickly I forgot the weather when that first fish struck.

When a heavy run of steelhead is in a particular river, fishing can be truly fabulous. At times like these it seems that everyone fishing suitable holding water gets into fish, and the action is frantic.

I recall one such morning in October on the Au Sable River, just a mile or so below the Foote hydroelectric dam which marks the river's upper limit for steelhead migrating out of Lake Huron. I was fishing with Don Weddle, a hometown companion, and our host was Gary Schnicke, a state-fishery biologist in charge of northeastern Michigan's gamefish program.

Gary fishes for steelhead as often as his job permits, and probably knows the Au Sable as well as any local angler. He suggested we fish a long, horseshoe-shaped run of fast water known as the Meadows. One side of the pool, on the inside of the bend, is easily waded and that morning was dotted with a dozen or so wading fishermen using spawn baits or Okie Drifters. We fished from the other side of the river, atop a 25-foot sand cliff with a brisk lake wind stinging our faces with blowing sand.

Oh, but the fish were in that day! It seemed strikes were coming within only minutes of one another, an unheard-of pace when you've spent long, fishless hours enduring cold and rain and wind as we had done the day before. I watched three anglers hook, play, and net handsome fish in as many minutes, and within an hour a countless number of others had been hooked and played, and most were landed. For a while the action was so fast that the angler's first indication of a strike was the steelhead's wild, magnificent jump free from the river, causing us to rear back on our rods and yell, "Whose fish is that?" One fish, which had to weigh at least 10 pounds, delighted in fooling us all by jumping and thrashing completely on its own, perhaps somehow sensing just how such behavior affected everyone's nerves.

Another avid steelheader is Bob Hume, a semi-retired bowling-alley owner who has for years owned a vacation cabin in Benzie County, a region which just happens to offer

Bob Hume and an average-size winter steelhead. This fish weighed 7 pounds, but some steelies come much larger. Note heavy clothing.

some of the finest steelie fishing in Michigan, on the Betsie River. Hume says without blinking that Benzie County "has the best steelheading in all of Michigan. When a man can catch half a dozen big fish a day when the steels are in, it's got to be the world's best fishing." During his forty-seven years of experience on the Betsie, Hume has backed up those words with an impressive array of truly impressive steelhead trout on hook and line.

His best fish as of this writing was taken during the Betsie's spring run and, unfortunately, was never weighed. But its measurements leave no doubt of its rightful place as Number One: A length of 41 inches and girth of 18 inches. Hume said the fish weighed in the neighborhood of 20 pounds, a very good fish even for the Betsie.

Hume's choice of tackle is determined by his belief that one day, if he fishes long and hard enough, he will meet the 25-pound steelhead he has dreamed about. His tackle is a heavy-duty open-bail spinning reel, 7-foot rod, and monofilament line of 17-pound test. His bait is almost exclusively fresh-cut spawn, which is fished on a No. 5 Mustad hook and a three-way swivel rigged with one or two No. 7 split shot.

Hume approaches his home water as do most successful fishermen: "The Betsie's natural condition is slightly colored, so you either know where the pools, the holding areas, are or you just fumble around. The way to learn the pools is to get on the water a lot until you know it." He could have added the advantage of seeking local advice near the river you plan to fish, and perhaps a few hours on the water with someone familiar with the whims of local conditions.

Fishing companion Bob Daily, who introduced me to steelheading on the Père Marquette years ago, had reason to appreciate Hume's knowledge one snowy afternoon in early spring. We had boated several miles up the Betsie to a shallow sandbar where Hume anchored and directed us to wade.

"The run starts about where that patch of willows is and continues down through here past that clump of trees," Hume said, pointing. "Let's each take a station along the dropoff and see what happens."

The first fish tapped Hume's bait without taking, and he quickly called Daily over. "There's a fish here. Drift your bait right through here and keep it as close under those willows as you can, and he'll take it," Hume directed. Daily did as he was told and hooked the fish, a heavy 11-pound male still bright from the lake, on his first drift through the run.

"There's no trick to finding fish if the run is on," Hume remarked modestly. "And this is a good run. If the fish are in, there's always at least one good one under those willows!"

Some people are just plain nuts over steelhead. Anglers I've seen waist-deep in the Père Marquette River hardly noticed a herd of deer which swam from one side of the stream to the other to escape deer hunters. The same fishermen seemed not to notice the whine of .30-caliber rifle bullets overhead when good fish were on. We're just nutty, the whole lot of us.

Bob Daily and I were fishing the Père Marquette near Scottsville, Michigan, some years ago and we'd lost two good fish in a row while beaching none. Thinking perhaps to change his luck by fishing alone, Daily moved downstream and around a bend in the river, out of sight but not out of earshot in case one of us needed help to net a fish. He'd been gone about fifteen minutes when the silence was shattered by a telltale series of sounds. What I heard from around that riverbend went like this:

SPLASH!

"Hey!"

Splash!

"Hey! A good one!"

Splash! POP!

"GODDAMMIT!"

That's the way it goes sometimes. Nutty, the lot of us. . . .

CARP AND CATFISH

For one brief, wonderful moment, I thought I'd found a bass fisherman's Valhalla. Fish—big fish—were breaking the water up and down the long riffle, their dorsal fins severing the fast water in the shallowest sections. But only for a moment. I was wading a section of a favored smallmouth stream in the month of May and, try as I would, there was no way those fish could be smallmouth bass. Quite a few of the fish moving through the riffle weighed well over 10 pounds, and the stream smallmouth record was less than half that.

They had to be carp, and Old Buglepuss was making his annual spawning move upriver into the wide, slow pools above. I moved quietly into the riffle to watch, but there was little need for caution. So involved in courting and travel were those fish that an elephant could have splashed across the river and not disturbed their frolic at all. Female carp, easily distinguished because they outweighed their male suitors four times over, zigzagged through the chocolate current closely attended by an entourage of four or more small males matching her every twist and turn, like fighters flying cover for a cumbersome B-17. Fish were all over the riffle, crashing into water willows, coursing beneath submerged logs, even dodging between the wader legs of an amazed onlooker still shaking off the disappointment of finding carp instead of bass.

I had no carp gear along, only light spinning tackle and a handful of ultralight plugs, so I stood and watched the show. Spring-warmed water temperatures were stimulating the carp to move into warm shoreline waters in search of the mud bottom and weed patches needed for spawning, and they were doing it in a big way. In the wide pool above the riffle, big female carp slowed their pace and began moving slowly through the shallows, followed impatiently by the male fish. Once a suitable area was located, more thrashing occurred as the fish prepared the site for egglaying and fertilization. After watching for perhaps an hour I shouldered my bass rod and headed home. This riffle would produce no bass today.

The common carp *(Cyprinus carpio)* is just that—common. It is today found all over the United States, though it is most populous in the eastern half of the country. The carp has a single spiny ray in its dorsal fin, plus sixteen or more soft rays in the same appendage. The lateral line contains between thirty-two and thirty-eight scales, and the scales themselves are quite large, often exceeding the diameter of a 25-cent piece. The fish's unlovely upper jaw has two "whiskers" or barbels on each side, used to aid in its search for food.

The carp is rather loudly adorned for so lowly a fish. Gold or gold-bronze is its predominant color, fading into olive or black on the back, and to a yellowish-white on the belly. Each scale has a black spot at its base and there is a dark rim around its edge.

North America hasn't always contained carp in its waters, but the species itself is quite old. In fact, the philosopher and historian Aristotle mentioned these fish as early as 350 B.C., and prior to A.D. 600, the Asian carp had been moved to Europe, where it provided low-quality food. But less than a century ago, Rudolph Hessel, a U.S. government fish culturist, decided America could no longer do without the fish, and shipped 345 carp by boat from Höchst, Germany, to New York City. The first stocking went into small ponds at Druid Hill, Boston. Some years later, Congress involved itself by distributing 260,000 carp throughout 298 Congressional districts. This act alone is to blame for today's infestation of carp in nearly every corner of the nation, to the detriment of sportfishing for other species.

Carp are bottom dwellers, for the most part. Their vacuum-cleaner mouths, aided by the four barbels, scour the bottom in search of anything edible, be it plant or animal. Carp muddy their environment to such a degree, in fact, that the resulting siltation has been known to suffocate the eggs of native gamefish. Water heavy with carp becomes permanently murky, reducing the feeding success of such stream predators as bass, panfish, and even catfish. During the spring spawn, sheer numbers and bulk of the carp population has been known to reduce the available spawning area for other species.

Little wonder, then, that carp have done little to endear themselves to fishermen seeking native species. Yet the carp is a fact of life over much of the continent and over the years has gathered about it a sort of brotherhood of fishermen happy to fish for large, strong fish which are relatively easy to catch and available nearly everywhere. To these tobacco-chewing, doughball-baiting, lunker-loving fraternity is this section dedicated.

There *are* small carp, just as there are small elephants and small mountains. But the rule of thumb for Old Buglepuss is big when compared to native fish species. Carp caught by American anglers probably average 10 pounds, and specimens weighing 30 pounds or more are not uncommon. Lake Erie has produced carp weighing nearly 60 pounds, but carp found in rivers and streams generally run a bit smaller than lake carp. The record carp in my home state weighed nearly 40 pounds and came from Paint Creek, a brook nearly narrow enough in places to leap over with a running start. The size of the water is secondary, to a carp's way of thinking, to its water temperature, gradient, and amount of available nutrients.

Carp prefer slow-moving rivers and streams with mud bottoms, although they are tolerant of other bottom structure, even rocks, sand, and gravel. The water should be either clear

How big is big? This catfish from a tributary of Brazil's Amazon River is more than 6 feet long, weighs 250 pounds.

or murky, weedy or barren, which gives some idea of the species' adaptability. The fish does well in pollution-killed rivers running through large cities, and seems to thrive where electrical generating stations dump heated water into streams. A spot on the Great Miami River at Dayton, Ohio, is one such place; large outlet tiles from the plant spew thousands of gallons of heated water into the river, and carp devotees come from miles around to catch carp here, even in midwinter when other waters are too cold.

Because the carp is a bottom feeder, this is where most anglers put their bait. Deadlining—fishing with no float or bobber—is often the best way to find carp. The weight of the line is dictated by the bottom type. A clean mud or gravel bottom allows the use of line in the 10-pound-test range, while river bottoms strewn with logs and other snags require line up to 20-pound-test. The rod and reel needn't be anything special, but the reel must be hefty enough to battle a tenacious and often superstrong fish of large size, and it must have a fairly dependable drag to combat the carp's famous tanklike runs. The rod, of any length suitable to cast prepared bait without flipping it off the hook, can be of solid steel, fiberglass, or whatever is on hand. Two-handed models are welcome when battling a particularly active fish in snaggy water.

Baits used for carp include just about anything a fisherman finds at hand. Carp feed by smell and taste, two closely related senses, and this is taken into account when choosing bait. Doughballs are undoubtedly the most commonly used carp bait, but the name is somewhat misleading because bread dough isn't always included. Slightly moistened breakfast cereals such as Wheaties are very popular. Bill Slivinski, a policeman by profession and a carp fisherman by preference, gave some surprising replies when asked what he uses for carp-bait recipes. Slivinski uses Wheaties which he moistens with a little water right at streamside before adding a teaspoon of powdered strawberry Jell-O. This is kneaded until firm, then shaped around a long-shanked No. 4 hook. Another favored Slivinski bait calls for buckwheat cereal moistened and shaped into a ball. No additives are needed, because the cereal contains its own maple flavoring. Some fishermen use cream soda instead of water, claiming the added flavoring makes a more attractive bait.

Whole-kernel corn is a popular carp bait. Be sure to choose the largest-kernel corn you can find, and bait up directly from the can as it comes from the store. Merely place as many kernels on a hook as it will hold. Some corn fishermen like to squeeze one or two of the kernels before placing it in the water, claiming this releases more "milk" into the water and attracts carp from a greater distance.

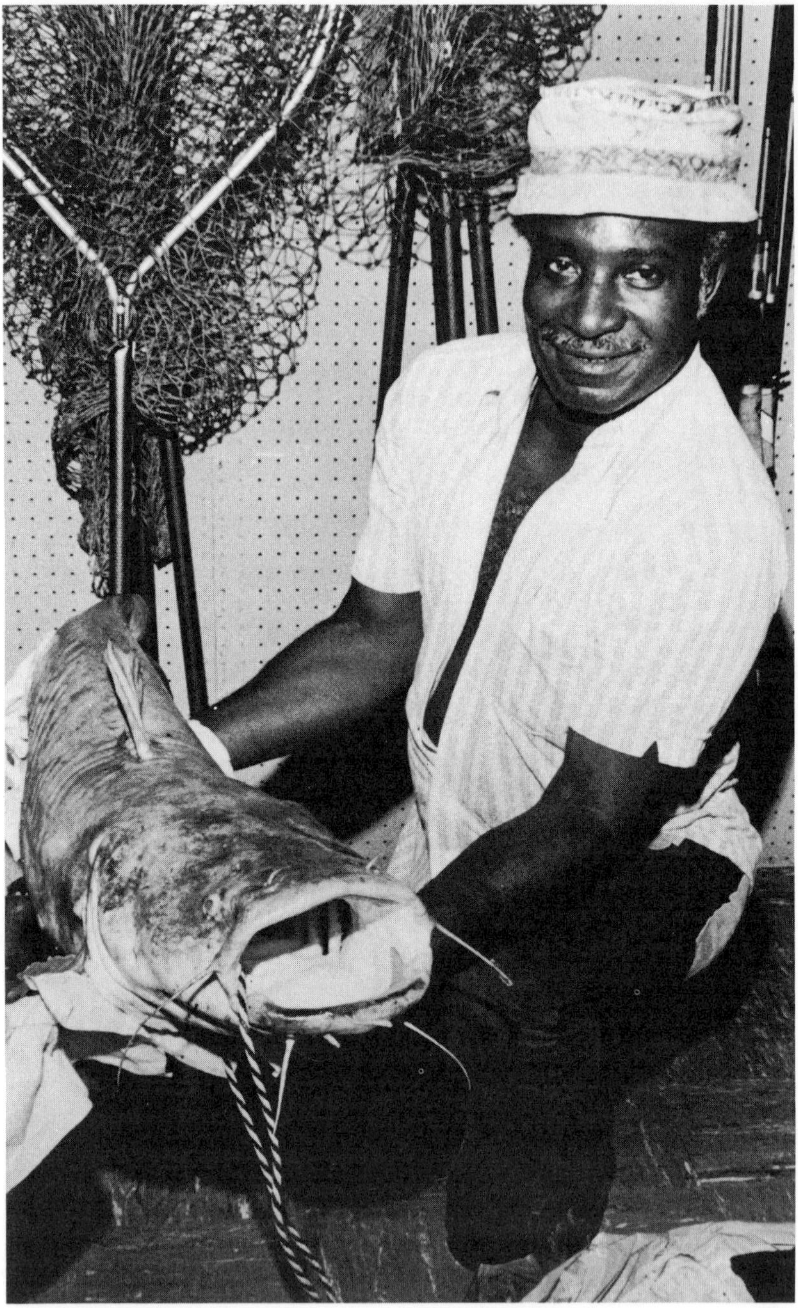

This catfish fell for a live minnow and weighed a bit over 62 pounds. Fish this size require heavy tackle and skill.

Carp are also caught on the standard live baits, such as redworms, nightcrawlers, and even live, large minnows. And carp have been known to strike the occasional artificial bait, as well. Harold Barefoot was bass-fishing a stream not long ago when a hefty carp struck the green Lazy Ike plug he was using. The fish took fifteen minutes to land and weighed 8 pounds. Later the same day a second carp struck the lure but was just too heavy to land on 6-pound-test monofilament line. In Kentucky, carp have been known to take poppers fished on the surface for bass and bluegills, slurping them in much like big trout.

Carp are not dumb, and sometimes require surprisingly careful rigging. It is, for example, a good idea to use a sliding barrel sinker when considerable weight is needed to get the bait on bottom. This method allows the carp to mouth and run with the bait without detecting a lot of weight on the line which could cause the fish to expel the bait and hook. When little weight is needed, try using just one or two split shot 18 inches above the hook.

Carp fishing is a sit-and-wait affair. The hook is baited and cast into likely spots, particularly where shallow water drops off to deeper water (fish the shallow side). Then the rod is propped into a forked stick and the angler sits back to contemplate the universe and maybe open a can of suds. Be sure, however, to leave your reel in the open or free-running position, because carp have been known to take a bait and run off with it quite suddenly. This means losing line, rod, and reel unless the reel is set so the fish can take out line. When fishing at night, detecting the first touch of a carp can be tough in the yellow light of a camp lantern or small fire, so here's a tip. Place a small bell attached to a short wire to the tip of your rod. The bell will sound when a strike occurs. Or you can pinch a pea-sized bit of dough to your line a foot below the rod tip. The light-colored dough is easy to see when the line begins moving away, yet falls off the line as soon as the battle begins.

Whenever the bite is detected, however, don't be shy about setting the hook. Carp have tough mouths, and it sometimes takes quite a shot to embed the hook properly. Wait until the fish pulls the line tight, then *heave* on the rod.

I'll bet most books and articles you've read about carp stopped short of telling you how good they are to eat. I suppose that's natural, because not everyone who catches carp goes to the trouble of preparing them for the table.

Well, that isn't the case here. The fact is, carp *can* be eaten, and a recipe I will relate makes them delicious. Start by removing the carp's head, fins, and tail, then scale the fish completely. Place the fish on a board of pine or some other softwood and garnish with salt, pepper, and cloves and bake in a 350° oven for two hours. Then just remove from the heat, baste with lemon and melted butter, throw the fish away, and eat the board.

There are, of course, quite a few serious recipes for preparing carp for the table. An early Ohio governor, Thomas Worthington, is said to have been quite fond of carp dishes and to have kept a supply in his Adena Estate smokehouse, along with prize hams. Here, then, are a trio of carp recipes, courtesy of the Ohio Department of Natural Resources:

Smoked carp. Grasp the carp by the tail and insert a sharp knife just ahead of the tail, removing scales in long strips, three to a side; remove head and all fins, split abdomen, remove viscera, and wash. Cut fish into uniform chunks from ½ to 1 pound each. Prepare a salt brine of cold water and salt strong enough to float a chicken egg, soak carp pieces for 24 hours, wash in clean water, drain and place on a wire-mesh tray in the bottom of the smoker.

Smoke over a hot fire (about 210°F.) for 2½ hours (fire should be of dry hickory, apple, or white oak wood); then add green apple or softwood maple for smoke buildup, and smoke fish for one hour at 85–100°F. After smoking cool fish before packing.

Polish carp. Ingredients: 4 pounds carp; 3 tablespoons butter; 3 tablespoons flour; 1 small onion finely chopped; 1 medium-size onion coarsely sliced; 1 pint dark beer; 1 or 2 pieces crumbled gingerbread; handful of raisins; 3 or 4 sliced almonds; red wine; sugar, salt, and pepper to taste.

Cut fish into serving sizes and boil in salt water until tender. Melt fat in deep iron skillet, add flour and small onion, and brown slightly. To this mixture add the beer, gingerbread, coarsely sliced onion, raisins, almonds, wine, sugar, salt, and pepper. Place fish on heated platter, pour mixture over fish, and serve immediately.

Cooked carp. Ingredients: 2 pounds filleted and skinned carp; 2 teaspoons salt; 1/4 teaspoon pepper; 1 medium-size onion.

Wash fillets in cold water and wipe with damp cloth, cut fish into serving sizes, place fish in wire basket of french frier, and immerse in boiling water. Season with salt and pepper and slice in one onion; allow fish to boil till well done. Remove and serve with melted butter.

CATFISH

It isn't tough to catch catfish. They eat almost anything, feed much of the year, and don't demand fancy tackle. In fact, the only objectionable thing about them is the mildly poisonous barb in the dorsal fin, a weapon I learned about early. It only takes one good stab with this hidden sticker to teach a youngster to handle any catfish with care.

The wound usually isn't deep or serious. It hurts for a day or two, bleeds a little, and then, given a good cleaning and some antiseptic, heals. An excellent way to handle the problem with cats up to about 5 pounds is to spread the index and middle finger of one hand wide apart, grasping the fish's two pectoral fins with the fingers while keeping the dorsal barb against the juncture of the two fingers. Even squirming catfish can be handled safely and securely in this manner.

Most species of catfish can live for amazingly long periods out of water, especially if care is taken to keep their skin and gills wet, something to remember when a mess of fresh-caught catfish is to be transported after a day's successful fishing.

The channel catfish is thought to be the most handsome and streamlined of all catfish common to North America, and this stream aristocrat does seem to be a bit more refined than its fellows. Unlike any other catfish, for example, the channel cat possesses both spots and a deeply forked tail, and the latter has given it the nickname "forktail." It possesses a total of

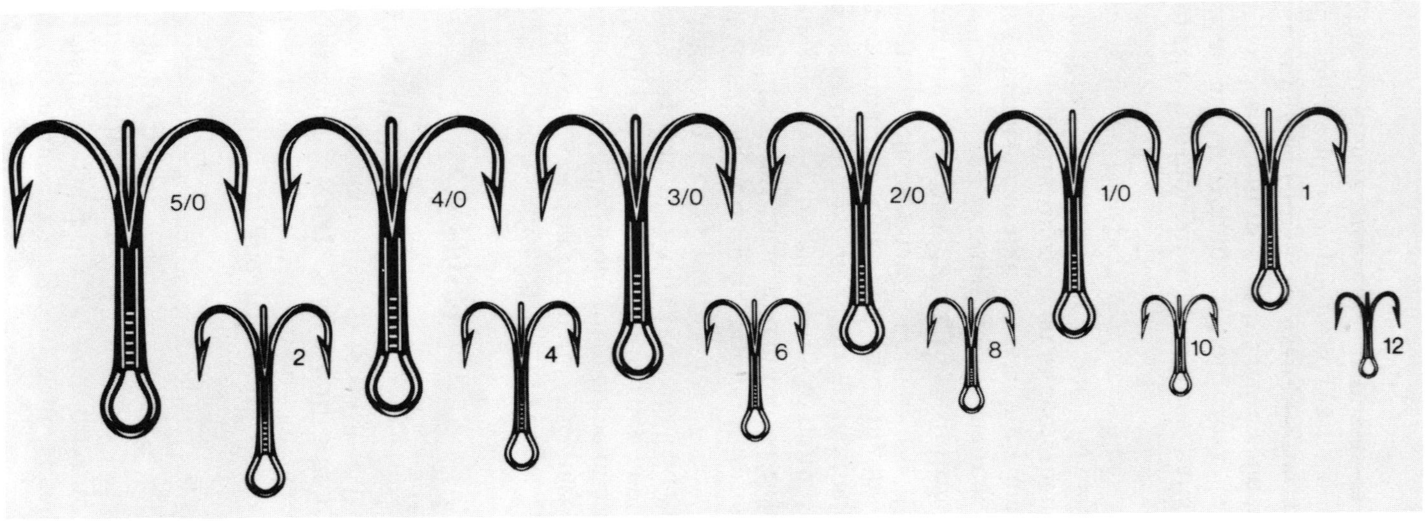

Catfish often take large globs of bait best fished with treble hooks to assure firm hookups. The size of the bait to be used will determine the size of the treble. Courtesy of O. Mustad and Sons.

fourteen separate barbels about the mouth, and the anal fin contains from twenty-four to thirty rays. The channel catfish's coloration varies a bit, but the basic color is a high-sheen silvery gray on the sides dotted with widely spaced black dots, a dark-olive dorsal surface, and a creamy white belly. The channel cat's original range stretched from the Great Lakes west into lower Canada and south to the Gulf of Mexico, but the species has been widely introduced elsewhere. It is considered one of the most common catfish species.

The channel catfish seems particularly well adapted to stream life because it thrives in a fairly persistent current and in fact uses the current to provide food. Forktails are known to feed just under the surface in the headwaters of pools just below riffles, cruising back and forth across the current in search of nearly anything edible. A favorite way to catch channels makes use of this slightly subsurface feeding method by using a limb line, consisting of a yard or so of strong fishing line tied to a tree limb closely overhanging the water. A hook is attached and baited with a live or dead minnow, crayfish, or small frog, and the bait is permitted to sway back and forth in the current overnight. If channel cats are present, it's a good bet the fisherman will find a self-hooked forktail on the limb line come next morning.

Jug fishing is another popular channel-catfishing method, particularly on the larger Southern rivers. A common bleach jug is armed with a few feet of baited line, tossed into the river, and permitted to drift downstream until a cruising channel takes the bait. The angler follows behind in a boat and retrieves the rig when a catfish has been hooked.

An old fishing compadre of mine swears the only truly sporting way to fish for channel catfish in small rivers and streams is with a long fly rod and a reel filled with light monofilament line. To the end he knots a long-shanked Mustad hook, and the bait can be a single lively nightcrawler, a couple of squirming redworms, a whole crayfish, or perhaps a live minnow. The angler wades into a riffle, lowers the bait into the current, and slowly pays out line. He claims the current delivers the bait right into the channel's mouth in a very lifelike manner, and has shown up at my doorstep to prove it, heavy stringer in hand. There's nothing shy about the fight of a 4-pound channel cat played on a light fly rod, either.

Channel catfish can measure over 30 inches in length and weigh over 15 pounds. They are firm-fleshed and excellent tablefare. Because of their liking for moving water, anglers fishing live bait below power dams, in slicks of fast water, take forktails in large numbers.

There are three types of bullheads—black, brown, and yellow—and together they probably make up 50 percent of the total catch of catfish, in terms of total fish caught annually in this country. They are certainly the most numerous and the least complicated of the whiskered clan.

The black bullhead *(Ameiurus melas)* is the only bullhead bearing spotted or light-colored chin barbels, and the only one with pectoral spines without serrations. The fish's color is usually nondescript—black to dark olive on the dorsal, lightening slightly on the sides and fading to soft white or cream on the underside. Like all bullheads, the black's tail appears almost completely rounded.

The black bullhead's original range was from New York west to the Dakotas and south to Texas, but the species has been widely introduced elsewhere, particularly where stream or river bottoms are soft and silty. An undemanding fish, the black bullhead is tolerant of both industrial pollution and warm waters and hits well on worms, crayfish tails, and meat baits, including beef liver and ripe minnow flesh. It seldom exceeds 2 pounds in weight and is a stocky fish which argues with hook and line in accordance with its small size.

The brown bullhead *(Ameiurus nebulosus)* seldom exceeds 3 pounds in weight. It can remain alive out of water by using atmospheric air for long periods of time. Another unusual feature is the row of rather sharp "teeth" along the rear edge of both pectoral fins. The body is a darkly mottled olive brown with darker brown markings, and the slightly fan-shaped tail is shallowly notched.

The brown bullhead favors large, deep pools of sluggish rivers and streams and seems tolerant of a wide variety of bottom types, although mud and muck bottom seems the favorite location. Natural diet items for this popular but undistinguished panfish include both plant and animal matter. Successful baits include raw meat, worms, diced liver, bits of marshmallow, and even wallpaper paste. Fish the bait dead on bottom with as little weight as possible for these plentiful catfish. The brown bullhead is found over most of the United States in all but the clearest and coldest stream waters.

The yellow bullhead *(Ameiurus natalis)* is only slightly lighter in color than other bullheads, but the lower surfaces of both head and body are light yellow to creamy white. The anal fin contains twenty-three to twenty-seven rays, and the rear edges of the pectoral fins contain small so-called teeth. Barbels are white or light-colored, and the body contains no spots. It is the only bullhead with a square, unnotched tail fin.

Like other bullheads, the yellow is found in slow-moving rivers and streams but frequents the shallower pools and shoal areas. Natural foods include snails, crayfish, insects, and minnows, and the species will eat a wide variety of the usual catfish baits. The yellow bullhead reaches a maximum weight of 3 pounds, with the average perhaps 2 pounds.

Here's a tip: The flesh of the yellow bullhead tends to become soft and mushy soon after removal from the water unless it is frozen or put on ice.

The white catfish *(Ictalurus catus)* has the reputation of feeding freely during daylight hours and reaches a weight of about 3 pounds. It has largely replaced the bullhead in the large, slow rivers where both exist.

The white's body contains no spots but is distinguished by the usually sharp color demarcation between the dark-blue dorsal surface and the rather starkly white ventral area. Like the channel cat's, the white's tail is forked. It is readily caught on such live baits as large minnows, live frogs, caterpillars, redworms, and nightcrawlers, all fished on or near bottom.

So much for the small catfish which are caught in large numbers all across the country. They are what you'll find in streams. However, just for the heck of it, let's move on to the big daddies which inhabit the large rivers of the South and Midwest.

The flathead catfish *(Pylodictis olivaris)* is one of the largest cats commonly found in the United States, sometimes weighing 100 pounds. Body color is several shades of dark brown. The fish's head is distinctly flat, with a lower jaw extending farther than the upper jaw.

The flathead is a denizen of long, deep, and sluggish pools on large rivers and is most commonly caught on trotlines and jigging rigs rather than hook and line. It is common from the Mississippi Valley south into Mexico.

Although the flathead is caught on a variety of meat baits, some of which have been left in the sun until ripe, the fish's natural food appears to be live fish. Big flatheads have the habit of lying perfectly still in shallow water with their cavernous mouths held wide open. Piscine passersby have been known to venture into the handy "cave" if frightened, never to be seen again.

The blue cat *(Ictalurus furcatus)*, another giant among catfish, appears to have been left with its eyes in the wrong place. The blue's eyes appear to be located in the lower half of its head, rather than near the dorsal surface as in all other catfish. Color is a pale to slate blue, and the tail is deeply forked. The current world-record blue taken on rod and reel weighed a hefty 97 pounds and came from the Missouri River in 1957. Missouri's Osage River produced a blue scaling 117 pounds, but the fish failed to qualify for the world record because it was taken on a trotline.

Like many fish and wildlife species, the blue has suffered under the burden of "progress." Man-made hydroelectric dams have choked the fish's beloved fast-moving rivers and reduced the species' numbers and distribution to a considerable degree. Today the fish can be found from Minnesota south into Ohio and the Mississippi Valley into Mexico, particularly below dams which discharge large amounts of water on a regular basis. The fish prefers rivers containing firm, rocky bottoms.

OK, so you've caught big blues from the waters of Tennessee's Pickwick Dam and maybe from the turbulent waters below the dams of western Kentucky. Want to try for something bigger, maybe a *lot* bigger? Then head south.

Several species of tropical catfish giants, called *valenton* locally, inhabit the tributary waters of the mighty Amazon River of South America. One species, called the *surubi,* is bright with a variety of colors and is said to leap as willingly as a tarpon when hooked. It reaches lengths of 6 feet.

Another giant is the hefty red-tailed variety, called *piraiba,* which feeds in the river shallows after sundown and can weigh over 200 pounds.

Closely related but much larger is the giant *piraiba,* which can weigh up to 600 pounds and measure 16 feet from washtub mouth to fleshy tail. Cats this size are sought with saltwater hooks and marlin rods, but even so the average fight lasts several hours from start to finish.

Well, the catfish has lured us pretty far downstream from the subject of this book, once we start talking about marlin tackle. But just in case you want to try for these South American giants, the best fishing season is from May through October in the area south of the Amazon, and November through February north of the big river.

How to clean catfish. As any kid with a willow pole and a can of crickets can tell you, catfish have no scales. Their skin is smooth and slippery and resists being removed from the tasty flesh beneath. But there *is* a way. My father showed it to me thirty years ago and in checking with other anglers I find the method in wide use today.

Make sure the catfish is in a demised condition. If cleaning time is at hand and the fish is still alive, rap it sharply across the head a couple of times with the dull rear edge of your knife. Then place the fish belly-down on a 1-inch wooden plank and drive a large nail straight down through the head and into the board. This anchors the fish during cleaning.

Then use a sharp knife to make a cut through the skin completely round the fish just behind the pectoral fins. Use a pair of dull-nosed pliers to grip the skin firmly and draw it slowly and smoothly toward the tail. If this is done correctly, the entire body skin should peel back in one piece and can be severed from the body just ahead of the tail. It's then a simple matter to trim away the various fins, slice each fillet from the sides, and discard the offal. Catfish, by the way, are top-grade tablefare, from bullheads to blues. I once had the pleasure of dining on catfish stew during a writers' get-together in South Carolina. Steeped in boiled tomatoes, chunks of potato, and seasoning, that stew plum guarantees I'll return there one day. I mean, it was *rilly* tasty.

ACCESSORIES MAKE IT EASY

If stream fishermen appear a little ungainly and maybe a bit bulky as they wade from one pool to the next, it's because they must have everything they need either carried on their person or stowed in some handy spot aboard their boat or canoe. Unlike the reservoir bass angler with his fiberglass bass platform with its dozen or so compartments, the stream wader either carries an item, or does without it.

For this reason, today's stream-fishing accessories are apt to weigh very little, to be easy to use and carry, and very often to do more than one job. They must be durable and dependable, because nothing is worse than discovering when you're a mile from the car that there's a hole in your landing net or that the small outboard on your canoe refuses to start.

CLOTHING

Any wading fisherman who uses a minimum of baits and other small pieces of equipment needs a place, or rather a number of compartments, where these things can be stored in some kind of order and where each can be reached with one free hand. The wading vest is the answer.

The vest is worn over the outside garment and therefore should be large enough to allow freedom of movement when closed in front. The vest is seldom if ever expected to provide warmth in cool weather and may contain a back panel of tough fiber mesh, providing welcome ventilation in hot weather. The cloth is usually made of tough canvas, duck, or cotton material with double stitching at all seams. All snaps, zippers, and button closures should be nonrusting, as all or part of the vest will most certainly get wet during a day astream. Modern nylon and synthetic zippers on all compartments do the job nicely.

The purpose of the vest, of course, is to carry as many small items as the fisherman normally uses. Many wading vests are chosen solely because they contain the most compartments, but this is only one consideration. If those pockets are not located so they may be easily reached, opened, and closed, and if the pockets are too small, the vest, for all its dozen or so storage compartments, is of little real use to the streamster.

Baitfishermen and flyfishermen will make use of the small patch or patches of sheepskin found on the breast section of most vests. Favored fly patterns may be safely carried here, and dry patterns are dried by the air between uses. Bait anglers sometimes carry spare hooks embedded in these patches, so that they don't have to dig in pockets and boxes when a hook change is needed.

Most wading vests also include two cloth tabs tipped with small brass D-rings, one on the vest's backside at the nape of the neck, another located somewhere on the chest section. The rear ring is used to tether the lanyard of a small hand net for landing fish, and the front ring carries fly boxes, hemostat, etc. A few models include a zipper-attached mesh fish bag in the rear, while others contain built-in flotation material in case of mishap.

An excellent way—and in my opinion the *only* way—to shop for a wading vest is to make sure the vest is tried on in the store before purchase. Ask yourself some questions: Is the vest easily put on, worn, and removed over winter clothes or raingear? Can you reach all the pockets and rings easily? Are the sheepskin patches large enough, and are they sewn or

There's no need to leave the amenities behind when floating the White River of Arkansas. Local guides use large, stable johnboats when guiding fishermen after the river's plentiful rainbow and German brown trout.

glued on? Check the zippers and snaps for smooth use and waterproofing. It's likely the shop that sells vests will also carry fly boxes and other gear containers. Borrow a few and see if they fit easily into the vest's pockets. If you will be baitfishing, does the vest contain at least one pocket large enough to hold a bait container (can of redworms, bottle of salmon eggs, perforated container of crickets and grasshoppers, etc.)? Choosing the vest that's right for you will pay off every time you get on the water. Take time and do it right.

A combination of canoeing and wading covers a lot of water but doesn't overlook hotspots requiring special attention.

So much for the top half. Now what about the bottom half, the part that goes in the water? Unless you wade wet, you'll need boots or waders that will keep your feet and legs dry and protected, yet permit enough freedom of movement to allow easy walking and stepping over those inevitable fallen trees at streamside.

Whether you choose hip boots or chest waders depends largely on the type of water you fish. A majority of anglers in our interior Western states equip themselves with hip boots because the streams in that area are small and shallow. Those few sections too deep for hip boots are simply bypassed. Hip boots are cooler to wear in warm weather and can be rolled down at the top during rest stops, while chest waders usually must be removed. I sure wish the wader manufacturers

Square-stern canoes outfitted with light outboard motors are mobile, handy and relatively inexpensive. This canoe is made of fiberglass, an excellent choice. Courtesy Mercury Marine.

would come out with a set of chest waders containing a waterproof zipper in the front. It would make getting in and out a lot easier, and make those stops up in the woods, well, a little less awkward.

I know three chaps who would have welcomed fast-removal chest waders one frigid April on Michigan's Père Marquette River during a spring steelheading trip. The three of us had been wading and casting for some time with no luck and a move was called for. With little forethought and less precaution, we piled aboard a keelless 17-foot canoe with a small kicker and moved off downstream, still wearing our chest waders and all clad in heavy winter clothes. In short order the canoe turned broadside to the current and over we went in a slick current deepened by a late snowmelt. They say you can't swim with your chest waders full of water, but I know three very shaken fishermen who did just that, clinging to streamside bushes until they could drag themselves, dripping and thoroughly chilled, onto the river's marshy shoreline. A nearby household generously offered us hot coffee and the use of an electric dryer before launching a powerboat to recover our canoe. And the canoe, which was *supposed* to float even when upside down, had developed an airlock that caused a vacuum that adhered the canoe to the river's sandy bottom and it had to be forced to shore like some reluctant whale. Go afloat in chest waders? You couldn't force me to do it again, not even at gunpoint.

I will add that had not Bob Daily reached dry land ahead of me and pulled me from the water, I might not be here. He may well have saved my life. Thanks, Robert.

Most chest waders sold today have three or more belt loops around the waist. The belted wader has two benefits; he is somewhat protected from filling his waders with water, should he take a ducking, and the belt provides a sturdy place to tether a stringer while in the water. Wading belts also help reduce that bulky feeling. Wading suspenders, however, do the job of keeping the waders in place. They differ from regular dress suspenders in a number of ways. The shoulder straps are broader and usually include a pair of leather strips or pads to ease weight distribution on the wading angler's shoulders. Clasps and fittings should be of quality, heavy-duty metals and leather, and the entire assembly should be tough and capable of taking repeated wettings without failure.

Chest waders come in two different types, stocking and shoe models. Stocking waders have waterproof stocking-type bottoms which are worn inside tennis shoes or specialized wading shoes. Shoe-bottomed waders cover the feet like high-topped boots and should have deep-tread soles for wading over slippery rocks. Some anglers add special wading sandals which are strapped to the feet and have cleats or rounded spikes. Some contain short lengths of chain for increased traction. But I am convinced, having used most of the available footgear, that a variation of Murphy's Law applies to wading, regardless of footgear: If you *can* lose your footing and fall in, you *will.* And have you ever noticed, while climbing back to your feet after a dunking, that regardless of how planned you try to make the incident look, everyone else on the stream thinks you're about as agile as a Rocky Mountain elk on roller skates?

Fishermen frequenting large, hazardous rivers sometimes use wading staffs, simple wooden affairs with a hard rubber or metal tip on one end and a leather loop, like a ski pole, on the other. This is probed ahead of the wading fisherman to tap the bottom for safe footing and also helps to steady the posture in heavy current.

The fishing hat is, judging by what I've seen worn astream, whatever suits the fisherman. Usually, however, the hat brim or bill shields the wearer's eyes from the sun, sheds a little water in case of rain, and offers a place where a lure selection can be toted out of the way but is handy. Good tackle shops sell sheepskin bands backed with elastic which are worn around the crown of the hat. The band totes a dozen or two flies or small spinners. You can, of course, get a little fancy. There are fishing chapeaus available which look like exaggerations of the hat worn by Sherlock Holmes with long bills fore (shields sunlight) and aft (keeps rain off the neck). Sensible, functional garb, no doubt, but I must admit to believing these hats to be a little humorous-looking when worn by some super-serious fly fishermen. Proper attire and all that, eh wot? Next thing, they'll be wearing English wool sports jackets and black ties.

THE PORTABLES

Besides the normal complement of rod, reel, line, and baits, stream fishermen amass and swear by an amazing array of items used for everything from removing hook barbs from fingers and fish jaws to trimming back fly hackle and gutting fish. The logical places for virtually all this gear are the wading-vest pockets, lanyards, brass rings, and maybe the canvas kangaroo pouch built into most modern chest waders. Each item has its own use and is an aid to the stream angler whether he wades or uses some type of watercraft.

Here is a probably not quite complete list of the basic gear that should be carried in the wading vest pockets, plus the intended use for each:

Lure receptacles. These may be fly boxes, fly books, or plastic lure containers with individual compartments. Most are carried inside pockets, but a few models include a clip attachment for carrying outside the pocket tied to a D-ring. Some containers are spring-loaded.

Dry-fly dope. Dope is usually a silicone liquid designed to make treated dry flies ride high. It is available in small bottles in which flies are dunked, and as an aerosol spray.

Nail clippers. These are used to trim knots and clip off frayed line and leader material; sometimes they have a pointed metal attachment for untying small knots, threading hooks, etc. I carry my clippers on an elastic cord outside the vest for easy use while wading.

Fly-line dressing. Dressing comes in a round, flat tin about the size of a silver dollar containing the ointment itself and a felt pad for applying it to the line.

Polarized sunglasses. It is wise to tether these with a foot or so of flyline to avoid loss. They are very effective for reducing water glare, enabling the fisherman to avoid obstacles while wading and to spot fish in shallow water.

Hemostat. A hemostat is a pliers-like surgical tool, usually made of stainless steel, that is very useful for removing hooks from fish and from the flesh of the less fortunate fisherman. Hemostats are available from medical-supply stores and some fine tackle shops.

Live-bait containers. These are usually for dry-stored baits such as worms, crayfish, hellgrammites, crickets, etc. Some models are strapped to the belt and contain a hinged lid, others are carried in vest pockets. All contain air holes and are made of either metal or fiber material.

Creel. Old-fashioned models still are constructed of woven wicker and worn on the belt or over the shoulder on a leather strap. Modern creels are made of sturdy canvas and nylon mesh with reinforced leather edges, and collapse when not in use for ease in travel.

Fish stringer. There are two materials used today, rope and metal. Rope stringers are sometimes preferred because they are lighter and can hold an almost infinite number of medium-sized fish. Chain stringers contain eight to twelve metal or nylon clamps which impale the fish's lower jaw or pass through its gills. If the rope type is used, be sure to tether it to the belt or boat with a quick-release knot, as the tethered end must be freed before a fish can be added to the stringer.

WATERCRAFT

There are occasions when even a dedicated wader like me will use a boat or canoe. Circumstances often demand it; sometimes the best fishing water is several miles from the nearest vehicle access point and you either run upstream in a fast boat or spend several arduous hours hiking overland. Then too, some streams, even surprisingly small ones, are best fished from a boat because of impassable shoreline cover, poor to impossible wading conditions, or currents and obstacles that make the proper drift of a bait possible only from some sort of watercraft.

Canoes. If a fishing situation calls for a choice between a canoe and any other type of fishing craft, I'll choose a canoe every time. It is quiet on the water, can be propelled through the water with a minimum of effort, and can negotiate surprisingly shallow riffles and fast water. Add a narrow keel and the canoe is amazingly stable; add a bracket to the stern of a double-ended canoe and you can use a small outboard kicker or one of today's improved electric fishing motors.

Modern, commercially produced canoes are made of one or more of four basic construction materials—fiberglass, aluminum, wood-and-canvas, and ABS plastic. Each has its merits and special problems.

Fiberglass canoes can be formed into almost any shape desired. Fiberglass is among the lightest of materials, is readily

V-bottom cartopper boats are probably the most popular fishing craft in the nation. Courtesy Mercury Marine.

patched, and, perhaps most important, is quiet on the water. A good friend of mine, Harold Barefoot, manufactures fiberglass models and created a specially designed model for his own use on the small rivers and lakes in his area. The canoe, of dull-finished green fiberglass, is 15 feet long with a standard beam of 34 inches. The canoe's height at stem (that is, at bow and stern) is only 12 inches, some 10 inches less than normal, and the gunwale height is only 11 inches. Instead of the usual 75 pounds for a 15-foot canoe, the special model weighs a gossamer 58 pounds. In addition, the craft has two rectangular blocks of Styrofoam just forward of each seat which hold fishing lures, plus a small hardwood shelf for dry storage of sack lunches, jackets, and, during squirrel season, a box or two of ammunition and a shotgun. There is also room under each seat for flotation material, although Harold's canoe is without this addition. U.S. Coast Guard regulations would require the addition of flotation if similar models were to be sold, however.

I have spent many an hour in this handy and comfortable little canoe. Its low profile obviously rules out use on heavy whitewater rivers or wind-whipped lakes, but I'd be hard pressed to design a better craft for the small, quiet rivers and streams we fish. Because of its dull paint job, the canoe can be festooned with a few leafy tree branches for jump-shooting waterfowl, employed at night on frog hunts, and, lest I forget, used as a dandy fishing platform. Whatever its use, however, the canoe's unusually low profile bow and stern avoid that irritation of turning in the wind.

Aluminum canoes are probably the most popular today in terms of their sheer numbers on the water. Aluminum is light and can be hammered back into shape if dented, although punctures are not as easily repaired as in fiberglass models.

ABS plastic canoes have been around now for several years, but some bugs remain to be worked out in this relatively new material. ABS plastic can be cast in whatever shape is desired, but repairs are difficult because the material is fairly brittle, encouraging hairline cracks.

Canoes of wood frame covered with treated canvas used to be all the rage, but they are heavy and rather unwieldy, can become waterlogged, and require considerable drydock time. Wooden-framed canoes are very stable on the water, however, and the large freight models used to carry amazingly large loads of furs, traps, and dry goods.

Johnboats. The johnboat is at its best on rather slow-moving streams where the boater has plenty of time to maneuver and the fishing situation requires little off-line travel. Johnboats are very stable, offer a great deal of storage room, and, because of their wide load distribution and shallow draft, can be used in shallow water. Their low profile makes them largely immune to wind.

Fishing buddy Jerry Sarver and I spent some fine days floating Indiana's Whitewater River in a 12-foot johnboat, using only a pair of canoe paddles for course adjustments as the current slid us past that stream's many bass hideouts. It was seldom necessary for either of us to step out of the boat when negotiating the Whitewater's mild rapids, and not once did we even threaten to capsize. It was made of aluminum, easily cartopped to streamside and then slid and carried to the water. This was a pleasant way to fish, casting to every bit of smallmouth cover in the best sections, then sitting back in the flats to light a pipe while the river carried us beneath riverside cottonwoods and past a well-remembered sandstone cliff which always seemed to host a hundred or so turkey vultures drying their wings after a morning bath in the river.

Today's johnboats (at least those commercially produced) average 12 to 14 feet in length with a 44-inch beam. They are sturdy and reasonably priced, and make a good choice for newcomers to stream and river boating in the market for solid fishing conveyance. Most commercial johnboats are made of aluminum.

Cartoppers. These handy and popular little V-bottoms are popping up everywhere, from the rivers of the East Coast to the murmuring streams of the Deep South and even on our big Western rivers. V-bottoms are sturdy, seaworthy, and available in almost any length and load rating. Their aluminum construction makes them light and tough, and rumors from several boat manufacturers indicate that even more developments can be expected in the future, such as all-aluminum bass boats with semi-V hulls and console control.

For the stream angler, however, the old-style 12- or 14-foot cartopper is still the best choice. They can be rowed or, if a bit of travel is needed, easily powered by an outboard of moderate horsepower. Their high gunwales and V-bottom make them more seaworthy than either the canoe or johnboat, and given proper horsepower aft they can make better time on open water.

The nice thing about cartoppers is their versatility. They can do double duty as stream craft and floating blinds during duck season, and they have the welcome capability of leaving the crowds of anglers behind when only those with powered boats can reach those between-the-bridges fishing hotspots upstream. Many a time I've had superb fishing all to myself in just this manner.

With the new emphasis on aluminum fishing boats, fishermen have a choice of handy features built right into the craft. Some of today's models offer dry storage in the bow and under all seat platforms. Most V-bottoms come with built-in flotation material plus the standard cleats and handles for easy tiedown.

The racks used for cartoppers are available commercially, but quite a few anglers prefer to design and build their own. The racks can be as simple as two 2x4 boards cut to the cartop's width and equipped with four large suction cups, two on each end. The boat's or canoe's weight helps anchor these racks in place while the rubberized cups prevent scratching the auto's painted surface. Tiedowns come in elasticized lengths and hold the craft firmly in place. A friend of mine has designed two-length sets of nylon-rope tiedowns equipped with rubber-covered metal hooks which are anchored under the auto's front and rear bumpers. Each tiedown can be adjusted for length, and they are quicker and easier to use than the old-fashioned metal-clamp affair. However they are fastened to the car, however, today's light, strong cartoppers are the cat's meow for getting afloat on river and stream with a minimum of time and effort. This is important when the craft is toted downhill and up through dense woods by a couple of guys anxious to get baits in the water.

Power units. Larger streams and rivers are sometimes best fished, and hotspots are more easily reached, if some sort of small outboard is added to the canoe, johnboat, or cartopper. Fortunately, today's marine manufacturers make a variety of such units available.

The small outboard kicker can run all day on a gallon or two of gasoline and has been improved. Shear pins have been eliminated in some models, starting has been made easier because of improved ignition systems, and increased engine housing has made operation quieter.

Johnboats and cartoppers in the 12–14-foot range usually

The wading angler needs the right gear at the right time. This fisherman wears good waders, fishing vest, polarized sunglasses, and a hooded shirt in case of chilly weather.

operate best with outboards of between 7 and 10 horsepower. Check the manufacturer's load and horsepower recommendations on the craft's data plate attached to the boat.

Double-ended canoes can accommodate either outboards or electric fishing motors with the simple addition of outboard brackets. Electric motors come in a variety of horsepower ratings and voltage requirements, and are much quieter in operation than gasoline engines. They can push surprisingly large craft at two or three separate speeds just right for moving through submerged debris or around bends in the current.

Anchors. The stream fisherman-boater has two uses for an anchor: It must hold the craft firmly and safely in a persistent current, and it must let the craft move downstream slowly when casting to shoreline cover is productive. Unless your stream fishing takes place in especially heavy current, there are two homemade anchors which will do these jobs just as well as store-bought models, and they cost a heck of a lot less.

The firm-hold homemade anchor is so simple you could make up half a dozen in an hour. Tell your wife to set aside the plastic bleach jugs when the contents have been used in either the 1- or 2-gallon sizes and fill each to the top with wet sand. Then coat the threads of the jug's cap with glue and tighten it down on the jug. This makes a sturdy non-snag anchor, and all that remains is to add a few feet of heavy line tied firmly to the jug's built-in handle. This anchor will keep a boat steady in all but the heaviest current and should last a long time.

Often, stream fishermen have need of an anchor which slows, but doesn't stop, downstream movement, and for this there is a homemade drag anchor. If anything, the drag anchor is even simpler to assemble. Merely obtain a few feet of heavy logging chain or an old truck-tire chain, add a length of strong line, and that's it. The chain is permitted to drag bottom behind the boat. Over most stream bottoms (save sunken tree limbs, for example), the chain should yield to the pull of the boat, yet keep movement slow enough to permit plenty of casts to those fishy hidey-holes along the shore.

The "brush anchor" is just about perfect for keeping a light boat or canoe tethered to sunken crappie brush or any other debris located in or near the water. It is reliable and quick to use, and available commercially.

ETCETERA

Snooping in another fisherman's paraphernalia is like looking into your wife's purse; you are *amazed* with what you find there. Fishermen are individuals, and although we all encounter roughly the same conditions when astream, each of us deals with them a bit differently. For this reason it is wellnigh impossible to offer a hard-and-fast list of items over and above the basics and exclaim, *This is what you'll need.* So here is a brief rundown on some of the extras I find useful. You can add or subtract gear as you please to fit local conditions.

Water thermometer. Since virtually every fish alive reacts to temperature changes in its habitat, knowing current water readings is extremely important for the stream angler. The more he fishes for such sensitive species as trout, salmon, and smallmouth bass, the more important such knowledge becomes.

There are several pocket models available which need only to be suspended in the water for a few seconds for an accurate reading. These are handiest for those who wade streams.

Boaters may use the same kind of thermometer or, because storage space in a boat is a bit more plentiful, use battery-operated electronic models complete with temperature-sensitive metal tips called thermisters. The thermister is attached to a length of wire which is lowered over the side of the boat. The electronic unit has the added advantage of enabling the angler to gain accurate readings at various depths, not just from surface water, although this is of little use in most shallow streams.

Landing nets. The purpose of the hand-held landing net is to capture the fish with one hand while the other manipulates the rod. Landing nets come in two basic frame materials, wood and aluminum tubing. Wooden frames are heavier than aluminum and generally contain glue and resins which can separate with age, but are preferred because of their aesthetic appeal. I have an old wooden net frame which hasn't been used in years, but I keep it around because I think it's hand-

Fishing in warm weather allows the use of the new one-piece fishing suit. It contains many pockets, is comfortable, and is machine-washable.

some. It also captured a lot of fish in its day, but I've moved on to aluminum.

The mesh of any landing net should be two things. It should be of quality material which resists snagging and tearing, and its pocket should be deep enough to accommodate the largest fish you're likely to hook.

Although there are many variations with the following size ranges, most nets seen today are of two general sizes. The so-called trout net usually has a cross-frame radius of about 14 inches and is either round or triangular with a rubberized handle. It usually has a 12-inch elasticized lanyard tipped with a snap clasp for attachment to a ring on the fishing vest.

The larger nets—those used for salmon and steelhead, for example—have a radius of about 25–30 inches and are usually round. They too are aluminum-framed and have handles 3–4 feet long with no lanyard. Waders usually tote these large nets with the handle down the back of their chest waders until needed.

Here's a tip: If possible, get downstream from the fish you are about to net. This allows the current to bring the fish to you and automatically opens the net's mesh pocket to its fullest. Also, try to net the fish head-first. "Pooped" trophy fish have been known to make last-ditch bursts for freedom, and netting them nose-first means that surge merely forces them deeper into the mesh. If possible, bring the fish to the net instead of vice versa; you'll lose fewer fish that way.

Cutlery. Knives are very much a matter of personal choice. Some anglers like belt knives, while others prefer pocket models. Whichever you use, however, it should be sharp, of stainless steel (nonrusting), and handy enough to be reached quickly. Heaven forbid that you fall in water over your head while wading, but should it happen you'll welcome the ability to quickly sever the straps and lanyards threatening to pull you down. It's happened.

Most knives, however, are put to more conventional work, such as gutting or filleting or gilling fresh-caught fish. And while you're at it, how about putting those fish leavings well away from the stream? Doing so keeps the water clean, and avoids misdemeanor citations by the conservation officers of some states.

Hook hones. Contrary to common belief, most lure hooks are *not* as sharp as they might be when the lure is new, nor are the hooks on lures or baits dragged over in-stream cover. A hone is called for. The hone weighs only a couple of ounces, fits in any vest pocket, and can replace rounded hook points with a real working point in a matter of seconds with only a few careful strokes. Just remember that hooks should be honed in a direction directly opposing the point. The same goes when touching up the hook's barb.

Here's a tip: Lacking a proper hone when astream, use the striking surface of any book of matches. It works.

Waterproof match case. The ability to build a warming, drying fire after a dunking has saved more than one life, as has a signal fire in case of an emergency, so it's a good idea to tote a dozen or so wooden matches in a waterproof container.

Here's one way. Melt a spoonful of wax and dip the tipped end of the matches in the hot wax to seal them from moisture. Then trim the untreated ends of the matches to fit inside the little plastic or metal cylinders used for 35mm film. These little cylinders come with tight snap-on or screw-on lids and will keep wooden matches dry and usable indefinitely.

Compass. There are several excellent pocket compasses available today; some are pocketed while others come with leather thongs for toting around the neck.

Neither type will help at all, of course, if you don't know how to use a compass in the first place. Read the directions and practice with the compass before you rely on it.

Leader unkinker. Monofilament leaders which remain coiled until used "remember" their coiled position and get fouled up on the water unless straightened before use. This is easily done with a bit of inner-tube rubber cut to 1x3-inch length. Merely double the tubing over the leader and squeeze while drawing the leader through your fingers. Do this a few times and most of the leader should be flat enough for use. You can also drop new leaders into boiling water before leaving the house, as this procedure, too, removes the "memory" from monofilament.

Camera. I don't know about you, but hardly anyone believes I catch good fish if I release same before showing the doubting Thomases. Maybe it's a flaw in my personality. At any rate, I like to carry some sort of small camera while fishing so I can record my catch, a set of strange streamside tracks, or whatever else strikes my fancy. There are a few good miniature cameras which fit any vest pocket and shoot cartridge film. It adds credibility when you plaster a photo of your big brown trout to somebody's nose and gloat, "See? I really *am* the best damn fisherman in the state!"

Just introduced recently is a packframe for 35mm cameras which puts the camera against the user's chest, out of the way when casting, climbing in and out of boats, etc. You'd have to take a full-length dunking to wet a camera carried with the new camera pack.

DOWNSTREAM— THE FUTURE OF STREAM FISHING

Nobody believed we would ever run out of passenger pigeons. In the late 1800s huge flocks of these tasty birds were so numerous that they blackened the skies and sometimes migrating flocks took hours to pass on their southerly route.

With the birds so plentiful and a ready market for their meat in the East, passenger pigeons were shot in incredible numbers. A favorite harvesting method was roost shooting, where hundreds of thousands could be killed in a relatively small area.

No one believed we could ever run out of passenger pigeons. There had always been passenger pigeons, there always would be passenger pigeons, and nothing man could do would change this fact. Yet today the species is extinct, a once-plentiful organism gone forever due entirely to the self-imposed blindness afflicting man when he is faced with a resource and a place to sell it.

They are a great deal alike, passenger pigeons and free-running streams and rivers. Each is unique, each is the product of a process beyond our capacity to duplicate, and each, once gone, is gone forever. No one ever built a passenger pigeon or a stream.

Shaver's Fork of the Cheat River, located in the Monongahela National Forest of West Virginia, is among the waters benefiting from a restriction on clearcutting. Courtesy USFS.

If we cannot create new streams, then we must do the next best thing and maintain what we have left. A survey of the problems facing that task shows the magnitude of the job ahead.

Michigan's Grand River, which mouths on Lake Michigan after passing through the large cities of Lansing and Grand Rapids, in 1976 received a massive dose of toxic copper cyanide from one of its metalplating industries. The poison, which passed through the city's sewage treatment plant undiluted, killed some 2,000 chinook salmon just making their way through the city's stretch of the river enroute to spawning grounds far upstream.

The cyanide killed at least a thousand salmon weighing 20 pounds or more apiece. Salmon this size are reported to be worth upward of $10 per pound in tourist dollars to the economy where they exist. The fish kill was therefore said to have amounted to $300,000 to Grand Rapids and the state of Michigan.

Coming upon a scene like this doesn't add greatly to a day's enjoyment on the water. The Izaak Walton League's Save Our Streams program is helping to eliminate this sort of blatant litter.

Chester Harvey, a water-quality engineer in charge of the investigation, expressed little hope of tracking down the source responsible for the chemical release and the subsequent fish kill. "It's wishful thinking to say we're going to nail the source on this. Grand Rapids has over forty electroplating firms. And all the publicity this has been getting hasn't helped, either. It [the kill] gets into the media and nobody wants to talk to us. Everybody clams up." Harvey said time works against the investigators in cases such as the Grand Rapids salmon kill. "Either we nail the source of the pollution within a thirty-day period, or not at all," he said.

The Grand, one of over a dozen streams on Lake Michigan to receive annual stockings of king salmon, lost 10 percent of its 1976 migration because of the cyanide spill. The city of Grand Rapids had to sweat out the fact that a major water intake valve downstream from the sewage outlet, where the poison entered the river, made contamination of Grand Haven water supplies a possibility. In addition, the cyanide's passage through city sewage treatment reduced the effectiveness of the plant's chlorination process. A state-issued announcement warned fishermen not to eat salmon caught from the river near Grand Rapids during the period soon after the spill. The apparently blatant pollution of the Grand River had effects a great deal more far-reaching than the killing of 2,000 king salmon.

Many chemical pollutions are far more insidious than the Grand River episode, however. A general cleanup on the Ohio River, from Pittsburgh to Cairo, Illinois, has brought sportfishing back to the big river and to its tributary streams. Fish species long missing from these waters began to reappear in fishable numbers, among them largemouth bass and sauger. Bass-fishing clubs chose these streams and the Ohio itself as sites for fishing tournaments and fishermen rejoiced: The Ohio River streams were back, gamefish were present with no threat of pollution!

But along came a quiet report from the Ohio River Sanitation Commission (ORSANCO), based in Cincinnati, that sent a cold chill up the backs of all the rejoicers. Sample catfish netted from dams at seven locations between Pittsburgh and Cairo showed dangerously high levels of PCBs (polychlorinated biphenyls) and chlordane. In making his findings known, ORSANCO director Leo Weaver said the chemicals' sources had not been determined, but added they probably came from a wide area rather than a single source. PCBs are widely used in electrical switches to prevent arcing. Weaver said he didn't know if the Ohio River PCB traces came from plants manufacturing the chemical or from those using it. Chlordane, which until recently was widely used in lawn-care products for insect control, came under 80 percent restriction by the U.S. Environmental Protection Agency in late 1975. "It keeps ticks and chiggers off the dog and the kids, but it runs off with the first rain," Weaver said.

Bill Klein, an ORSANCO biologist and its assistant executive director, said the two chemicals discovered by lab-testing the sample catfish are "hard," meaning they are nonbiodegradable and persist for long periods in the environment. "I would say this type of chemical would persist for months to years rather than days. They didn't occur overnight and they won't disappear overnight," even if the sources are shut off.

"Fish are great concentrators of chemicals," Klein added. "They [chemicals] may be in very low ratios in the water, but fish pick them up and store them in the humanly edible portions of their bodies, somewhat like the methyl mercury in Lake Erie."

Over a hundred bass-fishing tournaments were held on the Ohio River and its tributary streams in 1975–76. It is believed the same concentrations of chemicals found in catfish would also be present in bass. "We have no way to ban either commercial or sport fishing on the river, but the individual states have the authority to refuse to issue commercial fishing licenses and to prohibit the interstate shipment of fish for human consumption. About all we could do about sport fishing on the river is warn the fishermen of our findings," Klein concluded.

An addendum should be tacked to ORSANCO's assertion that the Ohio River and its tributaries have shown steady improvement resulting from cleanup efforts. Dr. David Stansbery, curator of the Ohio State University Museum of Zoology and an expert on free-flowing streams, says he has noted *no appreciable biological improvement* in stream-bottom samples since the ecology craze of the early 1970s. A few fish species may have returned in response to a better chemical makeup in stream water, he continues, but virtually no improvement in the numbers and variety of bottom-dwelling organisms which would be present in a clean, balanced stream environment.

Those meandering country brooks where that boy and his cane pole went to catch bullheads may not be around much longer, at least not as streams where the boy could expect to catch fish. Rural stream pollution originating on farms kills countless thousands of stream fish every year and often is the result of the farmer's refusal to adopt modern land-management techniques. Farm pollution can be divided into what the EPA calls point-source and non-point-source pollution. Point-source pollution is fish poison of one kind or another which originates from a single location, such as runoff from a livestock feedlot containing large numbers of cattle or hogs in a confined area. Non-point-source pollution includes

Industrial runoff from a plant near Springfield, Ohio, once filled the stream bottom with sludge. Public outcry finally forced the firm to clean up its act.

runoff from farm fields—fertilizers, pesticides, weed killers, and so forth—and originates from large acreages bordering the stream.

Feedlot runoff—manure—kills fish in two ways when in sufficient quantity. Once in the stream the manure becomes suspended solids; in amounts greater than 100 parts per million, the solids can clog the gills of stream fish and suffocate them. Manure runoff can also kill fish by greatly reducing the amount of dissolved oxygen in the water. State agricultural agencies say they are making slow progress in modernizing feedlot manure treatment; lot construction can also be altered to keep runoff out of streams.

Agricultural runoff is a tougher nut to crack, because the pollution source is as large as the cropfield's border at streamside. Outdated farming practices permit fertilizer and all the powdered and granulated and sprayed poisons farmers use to enter watercourses with the first hard rain. The most effective way to curb this runoff may be contour or strip plowing, enforcing a buffer zone between stream bed and plowed land, and vigorous law enforcement.

A state game protector and I were just about to depart his house for some bass fishing one summer day when a telephoned report of a local fish kill did away with our plans, so I rode along to watch his investigation. We reached the stream and immediately began to find large numbers of dead and dying smallmouth bass, rock bass, sunfish, suckers, and chubs. The game protector pulled on a pair of waders, entered the stream, and took a reading on the dissolved oxygen. It was well below the minimum safe level. Then he slowly waded the length of the stream's affected section, carefully taking notes on the number and type of dead fish. As all this went on, a farmer drove up and walked to the stream. Cautious at first, he finally asked what we were doing. The state man continued his survey but engaged the farmer in conversation. One thing led to another, and it soon developed that the farmer had applied the last of the liquid fertilizer on his fields the evening before. He then had driven his tank truck to the stream and hosed it out. The toxin had run directly into the creek, killing several thousand fish and landing the farmer in

Strip mining displaces topsoil, removes leafy plant cover and root systems, and bares acidic coal seams to air and water. Stripped areas are seldom returned to normal contours despite state and federal laws.

court. He was found negligent and fined according to the tally of the fish killed in the creek.

Municipal sewage also does its share to rob streams of good health and fishermen of their sport. The city of Piqua, in western Ohio, four times permitted insufficiently treated sewage to enter the Miami River, and four times a fish kill was noted. Finally, after five years' investigation, state prosecutors took the city to court and a jury found Piqua negligent in three of the four cases, setting the fine at $11,000, a mere slap on the wrist.

The fire-ant problem and its failing control program has for years endangered aquatic life, but there may be light in the tunnel after all. Mirex, considered to be the most persistent (hard) pesticide known, has been used in a failing effort to halt the spread of fire ants through the Deep South. A federal EPA ban on the product, unfortunately scheduled on a timetable not to be completed until mid-1978, will eliminate its use in the joint federal-state Fire Ant Control Program. It is possible that millions more acres of land will be treated with Mirex before the final phaseout is complete. The National Audubon Society led the fight against use of the chemical, and the EPA finally consented to drop further hearings and begin the phaseout in early 1977. The phaseout plan, ironically, was submitted by the state of Mississippi, owner of the nation's only Mirex plant, and sets dates by which various concentrations, uses, and means of application will become illegal.

Not all is grim, however. Among former President Gerald Ford's final acts was his signature on the Toxic Substances Control Act of 1976. The new law provides premarket screening authority to the EPA and phases out production of PCBs. Substances found to be questionable by the EPA may require action as simple as special labeling to a complete ban on production. Manufacturers can file objections and force test cases in court, and citizens can file suits and petitions calling for compliance with the act's requirements. This bodes well for the longterm future of keeping chemical toxins out of our streams and rivers.

THE TVA, THE ARMY, AND OTHER BEAVERS

Back in the 1930s, when the Army Corps of Engineers was the grateful and oh-so-willing recipient of the Appalachian Plan calling for the damming of troublesome rivers and streams of the East, flood control was reason enough to earmark millions of tax dollars for dams, and the Army complied. Then along came the Tennessee Valley Authority with an even better reason to choke off stream flow: electricity, jobs, increased tax bases, and a generally better life for a previously ignored section of the nation. Each mandate was to be an economic-recovery program designed to provide jobs. The Corps took the opportunity to dig into old files and dredge up all the programs originally turned down as economically unfeasible. TVA saw it as an opportunity to get into the dam-building business to such an extent that a self-perpetuating bureaucracy could be formed. Both schemes worked beyond anyone's wildest dreams.

The U.S. Army Corps of Engineers is probably responsible for the killing of more flowing water in this country than all the acts of God put together. Performing a juggling act with one ball labeled flood control, another labeled recreation, a third called cost-benefit, and still another called pork barrel, the Corps constructed earth and cement dams straddling waterways in virtually every state, and things don't appear to be improving much.

Case in point: Ohio's Little Miami River, the state's first-ever state scenic river and later its first-ever contribution to the national system of wild and scenic rivers, has three major tributaries. Despite state and federal protection of the main-stream, the Corps has all but completed dam and reservoir projects on two of the three tributaries, East Fork and Caesar Creeks. The East Fork fiasco will serve as bad an example as needed.

The Corps' claim said the dam was needed to avoid further flood damage following the flood of 1964. Flood control is a rationale high-sounding enough to garner federal appropriation dollars in Congress, through which Corps projects are funded. According to William Leegan, chief of projects and planning in the Corps' Louisville office, flood damage in 1964 from the proposed dam site downstream to the creek's mouth amounted to $366,000. A subsequent investigation by Jerry Jacover, counsel for a citizens' consumer-protection group, however, found that the Corps' estimate of damage did not stop at the river's mouth but extended for many miles down the Ohio River, the better to justify the $39.5 million price tag for the dam and reservoir project. A group of citizens whose property lay in the path of the reservoir conducted their own investigation and determined that damage from the flood of 1964 amounted to only $12,120, a sum hardly justifying a $40 million dam and the loss of virtually all of East Fork Creek upstream from the dam.

As early as 1971, county commissioners where the dam was to be built foresaw the need for an entirely new and modern

Unless municipalities stop dumping unwanted trash into handy streambeds, this could be the old fishin' hole of tomorrow. Courtesy Little Miami Inc.

sewage pickup and treatment system if the proposed reservoir's water was to be clean enough for animal and human needs. The sewage system was to be funded by many additional millions of dollars in federal money. That was in 1971 and no system has yet been built or begun, although the reservoir is scheduled to begin filling within two years (by 1978). Studies indicate that only a small percentage of the deep-water reservoir will contain enough dissolved oxygen to support life of any kind, and without adequate sewage treatment, none of the reservoir's water will be suitable for human or animal consumption. This is a dire prediction for a quiet stream described in the Corps' own environmental-impact statement (filed over eight months late) as "one of the finest examples of natural limestone stream in Ohio. The presence of freshwater mussels indicates the water quality is good, since this type of aquatic life tolerates little pollution."

East Fork Creek, southernmost of the Little Miami River's three tributaries, once provided truly excellent fishing for smallmouth and spotted bass, rock bass, sunfish, channel catfish, and carp. An Ohio State University researcher discovered gar in the creek, something of a rarity.

"As things now stand," said a newspaper account of the situation, "the Corps of Engineers is a frighteningly autonomous agency. The Corps decides which streams are to be dammed, makes up plans for the project, and then seeks adequate, if not inflated, federal and state funding for its busywork. The Corps is answerable to no one save itself, and perhaps an occasional Congressman who is willing to trade Congressional financial influence for votes in his home bailiwick. As Supreme Court Justice William Douglas pointed out, 'A member of Congress who is in good with the Corps will receive favors; those who may have been critical will be kept waiting.' "

The Tennessee Valley Authority, whose once-sacrosanct charter must now be questioned in light of the massive damage rendered the environment by its projects, is also not without blemish in the story of who does what to free-running rivers. Jobs and electrical power are its battlecry and longevity its goal.

Tellico Dam and Reservoir, at the mouth of the Little Tennessee River where it merges with the mighty Tennessee River, has been a battleground for years. Trout fishermen wanted the river left alone, claiming it was the finest natural

High-quality fishing must be watched after and nurtured. A local chapter of Trout Unlimited got their wish when the state conservation department tacked this sign near the Roaring Fork River.

trout stream in the Southeast; environmentalists and just plain taxpayers wanted the dam project halted to save money and to preserve the natural environment; and TVA wanted to build the dam as a part of its huge scheme for development of the Tennessee Valley. The battle was waged in court, in the press, and in national magazines, but in the end a federal district court in Cincinnati ruled in favor of the project, and the river seemed forever lost.

But where man failed, perhaps a small brown fish barely 6 inches long may yet succeed. A fishery expert from the University of Tennessee-Chattanooga discovered that the little fish eats snails off the river bottom and lives *only in that section of the Little T scheduled for impoundment by Tellico Dam.* The discoverer dubbed his find the snail darter *(Percina tanasi)* and after rechecking his facts, applied for rare and endangered species status with the U.S. Fish and Wildlife Service.

A FWS rulemaking issued in April 1976 designated the snail darter's habitat critical, a move which generally assures a hands-off policy by all other government agencies. This may or may not be the case on the Little T, however.

"Designation does not put a lock on it," says Jim Williams of the FWS endangered-species office in Washington. "A federal district judge (Sixth District Court, Cincinnati) has to decide whether critical designation of the snail darter's habitat is grounds to prevent impoundment of the dam."

Williams said a number of darters have been netted unharmed from the Little T and transplanted to the Hiwassee River, another Tennessee River tributary just upstream from the Little T. How these transplants fare in their new environment may help decide the fate of Tellico Dam, now over 90 percent complete and awaiting only a court release to close the locks and begin flooding the Little T Valley for some 17 river miles above the dam.

The Little T contains native and stocked rainbow and German brown trout, and closure of Tellico Dam will in a few short hours eliminate some of the best trouting on the entire river, maybe the best in the entire state. Once the dam is closed, as a hill-country old-timer once remarked, you can throw water on the fire and call in the dogs because it's all over for the Little T.

It must be added, however, that the federal government giveth as well as taketh away, and rare is the bureaucrat who is hesitant to point to the projects which have turned out well for both the government's and the stream fisherman's purposes.

A huge straight-gravity concrete dam and computerized national fish hatchery on the North Fork of the Clearwater River at Ahsahka, Idaho, is such an installation. Dworshak Dam and National Fish Hatchery is the highest straight-gravity dam ever built in the United States and second-largest in the world. The reservoir above the dam is 53 miles long. It was up this fork of the Clearwater River, some 500 miles from the Pacific Ocean via the Columbia, Snake, and Clearwater Rivers, that the steelhead trout used to come to spawn. Their path is blocked by the dam, but when the Corps built the dam, they also built Dworshak National Fish Hatchery.

Man and rivers can live side by side if care is taken to protect the river. This lovely trout-filled spot lies just a few scant yards downstream from the sewage-treatment plant at Aspen, Colorado. It is a flies-only section.

The hatchery boasts an egg harvest from wild fish of 9,600,000 eggs each May. The eggs are placed in trays and hatched until the fry have reached swim-up stage, then the little steelhead are transferred to twenty rearing ponds. By the following April 1, about 3.3 million young steelhead, averaging eight fish to the pound, are released for migration 500 miles downstream, where they grow to adulthood in the ocean.

Fish and Wildlife Service personnel operating the hatchery, many from nearby Nez Perce lands, have an enviable record for producing very impressive growth rates in waters controlled by Suzie, a huge computer whose job it is to monitor and control water flow, pond and tank temperatures, feeding schedules, and other hatchery chores. Just making up a menu would have to stagger even the best worker; the hatchery feeds its trout 630,000 pounds of food a year.

Cooling towers, their bases' diameters greater than the length of a football field, are required to return river water to its original temperature. Courtesy TVA.

In addition to steelhead, Dworshak raises rainbow and cutthroat (native) trout, and kokanee salmon. These fish are released either directly into Dworshak Reservoir or its many tributary streams.

Depending on who you ask, then, the Dworshak Dam and Hatchery is either a good or a bad thing. Government people point with justifiable pride to the huge fish production and increased fish growth achieved by Dworshak. Fishermen with a narrower view of the idea of fishing for hatchery-raised trout might wish the infernal thing had never been built and they still could catch native steelhead born in the high country gravel beds far above the present damsite, beyond which no steelhead ever swims today.

Although he was undoubtedly thinking in terms of dollar savings rather than sportfishing, former Director Bill Nye, of the Ohio Department of Natural Resources, forever endeared himself to Ohio stream fishermen in the early 1970s by deactivating no fewer than thirty-one Corps of Engineers projects in Ohio. Among the halted projects were major dams, channelizations, and other stream-ruination boondoggles. Nye left office when his boss, former Governor John J. Gilligan, lost a close election to Jim Rhodes. Nye's replacement, agronomist Dr. Robert Teater, formerly of Ohio State University, will have to show more than he has to date to curry the sportsmen's favor as did Bill Nye. Teater, by the way, spent his first twenty-two months in office without the official approval or confirmation of the state senate, a mark of wise caution not often seen in the legislative branch of that state.

Drowning a stream in its own water isn't the only way to do away with it, however. You could always drive a steam shovel right up the stream bed, widening its banks to a uniform measure, lowering and broadening its water level, and scraping away every living plant and animal—including fish—in the stream.

You could do that if you wanted to. You might as well. The U.S. Soil Conservation Service, its state counterparts, and federal and state highway departments have been doing it for many years.

It's called channelization, and it is without a doubt the ugliest, most destructively long-lasting practice ever to destroy good fishing water.

It starts when landowners decide that rainwater isn't draining off their property fast enough. Perhaps outdated farming methods permit spring rains to take valuable topsoil off the fields and into the stream, where it is swept downstream to fill in pools and clog riffles. Perhaps farmers would rather call in government bulldozers and engineers than keep plowed earth a safe distance from spring flood limitations.

Whatever the reason (SCS, like Milton Berle, has a million of 'em), channelization does several things to a stream. Heavy equipment is used to broaden and straighten the stream bed to a uniform width and depth. Shoreline cover, such as willow thickets, overhanging trees, fallen logs, and brushpiles are scraped away so that nothing remains to slow the water's passage off the land or provide shade. There are no more pools or riffles, no more undercut banks and sure-bet trout hide-

An abandoned strip mine slowly fills with acid water. Left alone, such pools often spill over, polluting nearby watercourses. This scene is in Lawrence County, Ohio, in the Wayne National Forest.

outs. There is only a sterile ditch with the telltale tracks of cleat-footed heavy equipment punched into the grass between stream and roadside.

The irony of the policy of channelization lies in attempts to revitalize the stream ten, twenty, even thirty years later. Trees may have grown back (if the dozers left enough topsoil), and perhaps a few logs have fallen into the water, creating very small pocketwater where a few fish cling. By and large, however, a stream channelized today will still be essentially sterile dozens of years down the road, and attempts to alter this condition cost the taxpayer many dollars on top of the original cost of the project. It costs money to buy equipment and send crews to the stream with orders to construct gabions and wing deflectors and other structures which interrupt the current enough to create fish habitat. It costs money to replant shorelines denuded of all plant life by bulldozers. And it takes a lot of time for shoreline and aquatic plants to reach sufficient growth and density to support the microscopic life where all stream life begins in the food chain and the production of oxygen.

The shorelines of this small stream have been rutted and eroded by cattle permitted to graze right up to the water's edge. Manure runoff also could be a problem here.

And once in a great while, one of the grandiose channelization projects, so highly touted for getting all that nasty water off the land, backfires and plain doesn't work. A family I know lives in Athens, Ohio, in the hill country of the state's southeastern section. A federally funded channelization of the sizable Hocking River nearby was so well done, so well

A state game protector follows up a fish-kill complaint by testing the water for dissolved oxygen. This single pollution instance killed over 60,000 stream fish.

engineered, that it received a national engineering award from the Corps of Engineers. But a funny thing happened when the project was completed and the river was supposedly tamed. Heavy spring rain came, flash floods popped up all over the region, and the family's house and two of its members were very nearly swept away by a wall of water the *improved* river channel failed to contain. It would be funny if it hadn't very nearly been tragic.

Don't give up on the future of stream fishing just yet. There's more to come.

Another way to destroy your favorite bass stream is to give it a healthy and continuing shot of sulfuric acid, a mixture of coal, air, and water guaranteed to kill off every living organism it touches. We're doing exactly that every time we allow a mining company to walk away from a strip, drift, or deep mine without fully and adequately reclaiming the land.

Want examples? Boy, do I have examples.

An old and long-abandoned deep mine in the Wayne National Forest is now seeping and probably always will seep a healthy supply of blood-red acid water because when the coal ran out the mining company, as permitted by the lax laws of the era, merely pulled up stakes and moved away. It had its profit, no voice was raised in opposition, and who cared about a little old hole in the hill, anyway? It didn't take long for groundwater to begin seeping into the cavity in the ground, at the same time passing over exposed remnants of a coal vein and turning into discolored sulfuric acid. The water built up until finally it spilled out the mouth of the old mine, burning a path for itself through surrounding forest vegetation until it reached the nearest creek. Like fingers of death the acid moved downstream, destroying life wherever it was contacted.

Raccoon Creek, probably one of the loveliest streams in the lower Midwest, runs between wooded ridges, passes through a state forest, and is surrounded by wild terrain holding whitetail deer, ruffed grouse, quail, and songbirds. The creek water is extremely clear and runs over clean gravel unfettered by moss, watercress, or other aquatic plants. Raccoon Creek is lovely, clean as can be—and dead, the victim of long-term poisoning from many abandoned strip and deep mines in its watershed. State and federal officials infrequently make gestures to placate public complaints about poisoned streams resulting from mining operations, but no technology yet tried can shut off the faucet of acid. Once opened, it is like a door to hell which cannot be closed.

Clearcutting (Forest Service people prefer the Sunday-go-to-meeting term "even-aged management") can be a good or bad tool, depending on where and how it is used. Clearcutting is the total denuding of a predetermined tract of land of every plant above a few inches in height. This is done with motorized timber-harvesting equipment and opens up large tracts of formerly forested land to the elements. Selective cutting calls for marking and cutting only those trees in a stand which meet size and quality minimums. This harvest method removes the largest trees, thins the forest, and permits some secondary growth to occur. Robert Rankin, a forester on the Aspen District of the immense White River National Forest, Colorado, explained the decision of whether to use clearcutting or selective cutting depends on terrain and soil type.

"We can clearcut safely on surprisingly steep terrain if the soils are right," he said. "Good soil can withstand the removal of live root structure without sliding, even on mountains so steep we have to use balloon lifts to get the timber off the mountain. In other places we know the soil just won't stand a heavy timber cut without slipping, and we either leave some of the trees or don't cut at all." This is especially important on Western forests where topsoil is thin and snowmelt is seasonally heavy.

But although the Forest Service and some commercial timber growers have in some cases adopted improved timbering methods, some large tracts on terrain far too steep are still clearcut, which removes the soil's stabilizing plant roots and the leafy overstory that shields the soil from the full force of rainfall. Heavy rain loosens the now-vulnerable topsoil, washing it into the nearest watershed, where it can and does fill up another fishing stream as a child fills a bucket with sand. West Virginia residents and conservation groups made their fight against clearcutting stand up, and the practice is now restricted in that state's Monongahela National Forest, so it *can* be regulated by a vigilant public.

Thermal pollution—the overheating of streams and rivers by using them as disposals for superheated cooling waters of fossil-fuel (coal) and nuclear generating plants—can be expected to be a continuing problem until a process known as once-through cooling is a thing of the past.

Once-through cooling refers to the number of times an amount of coolant—in this case water from nearby rivers—is used in the plant's cooling process before being discharged

A half-finished stream channelization leaves its ugly signature: Bulldozer tracks from water to roadside. This site is located in Logan County, Ohio.

back into the river. Overheated discharge raises the river's temperature for amazing distances downstream from the plant's outlet, as attested by infrared photos which show the telltale plume of heat extending for 20 miles or so. The electrical industry's PR types will sell you the story that heated water is good for the fisherman because it often attracts large numbers of fish in cold weather, but this ploy is only partly

Sludge from the bottom of a tributary stream into which International Harvester dumped its plant effluent. Such water does not support many trout.

true. Fish *are* attracted by the plant's heated water, particularly when the river itself is cold, but aquatic scientists say that warm water in midwinter completely eradicates some species of aquatic animals while throwing out of sync the reproductive cycles of others. Disturbing the normal winter regenerative period of a river is like keeping a man awake for twenty-four hours and expecting him to function at full capacity. It cannot be done.

The future of streams and stream fishing appears grim indeed when viewed through the not-so-rosy glasses of the problems touched on here. Let's face it: The future *is* grim, but not without its glimmers of hope.

The streams which are clean and fishable fifty years from now will be that way because common folk laid their ears back and forced the politicians and industries and bureaucracies to forget the almighty buck long enough to realize that continued failure to heed the clamor for clean streams and rivers would be the worst possible public-relations blunder, the kiss of death for a marketed product or votes in the home district. For their part, consumers may have to pay more in taxes while doing without pork-barrel spending programs. Some groups are already doing that.

The Izaak Walton League of America has a program for citizen participation in stream preservation. Called Save Our Streams, with the appropriate initials SOS, the program urges local groups of IWLA members to adopt streams near home, seek government help in eliminating pollution sources, and organize cleanup projects. IWLA's Garden of the Gods Chapter of Colorado Springs is doing just that, as reported in *Outdoor America*, the League's monthly publication.

The chapter adopted Fountain Creek and began investigating the how and where of getting the stream cleaned up. IWLA national secretary Helen Stammen, also the chapter's secretary, explains how they did it.

"Because I had worked with the previous mayor of Manitou Springs and knew about the city's interest and concern about litter and pollution, I approached Mrs. Russel Paul, a Manitou councilwoman, about adopting a portion of Fountain Creek which goes through the city. She thought the idea was great and had a resolution drawn up. It was presented and adopted by the city council," Stammen said.

That started the cleanup program. "In Colorado Springs, the main polluter was a car wash. All the soap and dirt were drained directly into Monument Creek (another adopted stream). We contacted the Colorado Water Pollution Commission and it has been cleared up." A local Boy Scout troop pitched in with the cleanup effort, earning conservation badges for their participation. Special effort was made to get local news media involved so that the chapter's efforts would be put before as many people as possible.

The Baltimore County SOS program in Maryland has opened five collection centers for used automotive oil in an effort to keep this pollutant out of storm sewers and drains, where it eventually reaches local streams. Collected oil is taken to refining plants for recycling, and the project has a possible annual capacity of 5 million gallons of used oil, the amount handled by do-it-yourself mechanics in Maryland every year.

Information on IWLA's Save Our Streams project is available by contacting the IWLA National Office, 1800 N. Kent St., Suite 806, Arlington, Va. 22209.

I for one like to think there will be streams to fish and gamefish to catch for a long time to come, given enough attention to and care for the streams themselves. I think streams are special enough to keep around and kind of hope when my number is called I'll stand before the Pearly Gates unabashedly dressed in a set of chest waders still dripping water from my favorite stream. See you on the water.

INDEX

Boldface numbers refer to illustrations